CRIMINAL PROCEDURE IN
NORTH CAROLINA

*The University of North Carolina Press, Chapel Hill, N. C.;
The Baker and Taylor Co., New York; Oxford University
Press, London; Maruzen-Kabushiki-Kaisha, Tokyo; Edward
Evans & Sons., Ltd., Shanghai.*

CRIMINAL PROCEDURE IN NORTH CAROLINA

As Shown by Criminal Appeals Since 1890

BY

GEORGE RAYMOND SHERRILL, Ph.D

Associate Professor of History and Economics, Clemson Agricultural College, Clemson College, South Carolina

CHAPEL HILL
THE UNIVERSITY OF NORTH CAROLINA PRESS
1930

PRINTED IN THE UNITED STATES OF AMERICA BY
THE SEEMAN PRESS, DURHAM, NORTH CAROLINA

TO MY

FATHER AND MOTHER

PREFACE

IN RECENT years there has been an increasing amount of criticism of the state courts in this country. Without venturing an opinion as to whether this criticism is justified, it is a fact that much of the discussion has been based on individual cases rather than upon the judicial process as a whole. In order to make an accurate appraisal of the work of the courts, it is necessary to consider all the cases decided for a considerable period of time. This book is an attempt to analyze a sufficient number of cases decided by the courts of the state to show the general trends and tendencies in the interpretation by the Supreme Court of criminal procedure.

On account of the complex and involved character of the problems in the Social Sciences and in Law, research must of necessity be regional and intensive rather than broad and general. This monograph is presented as a regional study in the actual functioning of the courts of North Carolina in the trial of criminal cases.

I am indebted to Professor Raymond Moley of Columbia University for many valuable suggestions. My thanks are due Chief Justice Walter P. Stacy and the Associate Justices of the Supreme Court of North Carolina for conferences and suggestions. Assistant Attorney General Frank Nash gave valuable information and permitted the use of his records in the preparation of the statistical portion of the study. Mr. Edward Seawell, Clerk of the Supreme Court, provided me with the briefs that have been filed in his office by counsel. Professor A. C. McIntosh of the University of North

Carolina Law School and Dr. N. Y. Gulley, dean of Wake Forest College Law School, gave much friendly help and advice. Judge Hugo Grimm of St. Louis, Missouri, and Honorable J. C. B. Ehringhaus of Elizabeth City, North Carolina, favored me with helpful letters. Professor John B. Waite of the University of Michigan read my manuscript and made suggestions. Professors H. W. Odum, Roy M. Brown, and Miss Mary Thornton did much to facilitate and assist me with this study. Finally, my thanks are due the University of North Carolina for extending to me the courtesies of a visiting student and supplying me with much of the material which I have used.

GEO. R. SHERRILL

Clemson College
South Carolina

TABLE OF CONTENTS

CRIMINAL PROCEDURE IN
NORTH CAROLINA

CHAPTER I

THE NORTH CAROLINA JUDICIAL SYSTEM

THE PURPOSE of this study is to make an analysis of the criminal cases that have been disposed of by the Supreme Court of North Carolina from 1890 to 1927 inclusive. Taking the Supreme Court as the standard, and assuming that its decisions and opinions are expressive of the law, one can get some idea of what is happening in the courts below by its action in affirming or reversing the decisions of the lower courts. Such a study is of necessity limited in its scope and includes only a small percentage of the total cases tried in the state. During this period 423,509[1] criminal cases were disposed of by the Supreme Courts of the state but only 1,842 were finally carried through the Supreme Court, thus giving .4 of one per cent of the total number of cases to be considered in this study. While the number of cases appealed is relatively small, they are very important. The great majority of criminal cases are finally disposed of in the lower courts. The defendant is either satisfied or feels that he could not profit by an appeal, if there is sufficient ground for taking one. But there are many complicated cases, involving intricate points of law and legal technicalities, about which there might well be an honest difference of opinion, and these are the cases most often appealed to the Supreme Court.

An analysis of the cases of course requires information as to the total number of cases appealed, the number of appeals dismissed, the number of cases af-

[1] *Biennial Reports of the Attorney General of North Carolina,* Raleigh, 1890-1926.

firmed, the number reversed and remanded and the number reversed. It is necessary to know something of the character of the cases appealed, the nature of the offense charged, the grounds for taking the appeal, the action of the appellate court in disposing of the points made on appeal and the final decision upon the case.

Since this study is of a technical nature and since there is considerable variation in the several states of the Union in the organization and procedure of the lower courts, it seems that a brief explanation of the different courts of the state and of criminal procedure might be helpful to an understanding of the subject. This outline contains a brief descriptive discussion of the Supreme Court, the Superior Courts, Courts of Justices of the Peace, Recorders Courts and County Courts. There is also a brief discussion of the more recent compilations of statutes in the state.

THE SUPREME COURT

A full and exhaustive history of the Supreme Court of North Carolina has never been written. However, 103 N. C. 309 (1890), contains an address on the History of the Supreme Court delivered in Raleigh February 4, 1889, in commemoration of the First Occupancy by the Court of the New Supreme Court Building, by Honorable Kemp P. Battle. His opening sentence says, "In tracing the history of the Supreme Court of North Carolina, we find that its origin is not the Act of 1818, which established it on its present basis, but that it properly begins with the first organized government in our state." With great care the speaker follows the successive struggles through which the Court finally evolved.

177 N. C. 617 (1919), contains a History of the Supreme Court of North Carolina by the late Chief Justice Walter Clark.[2] Particular emphasis is placed on the period after 1889. Chief Justice Clark said in part:

The Constitution of 1776 provided that the General Assembly should by joint ballot appoint judges of the Supreme Court who should hold office during good behavior. The General Assembly seemed to consider that, there being no appellate court, the Superior Court filled this requirement, for there was no appellate court until one was created in 1799, consisting of all the Superior Court judges, to continue for one year, the object being to try James Glassgow, Secretary of State, and others for fraud in the issuance of land scrip in Tennessee to Revolutionary soldiers. At the expiration of one year the act was continued in force by chapter 12, Laws 1801. . . .

This court was styled the "Court of Conference." In 1804 the court was required to file written opinions, and in 1805 the title was changed to the "Supreme Court," a tardy recognition of the constitutional provision of 1776. . . .

In 1810 the judges hearing appeals in conference were authorized to elect a Chief Justice, and John Louis Taylor was the first and only judge to fill that position. A seal and a motto were directed to be established by the court and the right of appeal was prescribed. Any two judges of the six, sitting in conference at Raleigh, were a quorum.

In November, 1818, the Supreme Court contemplated forty-two years before by the Constitution of 1776, was at last created by legislative enactment. . . . The salary of the judges was fixed at $2,500 each, the salary of the Governor at that time being $1,900, and the salary of the Su-

[2] Walter Clark, "History of the Supreme Court of North Carolina," 177 N. C. 619-20 (1919).

perior Court judges, previously $1,650, was raised to $1,800. The judges of the Superior and Supreme Courts were elected by the Legislature and held for life till 1868, when these courts were created in the Constitution, without liability of abolishment by the Legislature as formerly, and the judges were made elective by the people for a term of eight years.

The constitutional provisions relating to the organization and powers of the Judicial Department are contained in Article IV of the state Constitution which was adopted in 1868. The organization of the Supreme Court is pretty fully set forth in the following sections and statutes.

The Constitution, Article IV, Section 2, provided that the judicial power of the State shall be vested in a Court for the trial of impeachments, a Supreme Court, Superior Courts, Courts of Justices of the Peace, and such other courts inferior to the Supreme Court as may be established by law.

The number of justices, method of election and terms of office are fixed by the Constitution.[3] The Court consists of a Chief Justice and four Associate Justices. They are elected by the qualified voters of the state in the same manner as is provided for the election of members of the General Assembly, and they hold office for eight years.[4]

The jurisdiction of the Supreme Court is provided for in Sections 8 and 9. Section 8 prescribes the appellate jurisdiction and reads as follows:

The Supreme Court shall have jurisdiction to review, upon appeal, any decision of the courts below, upon any

[3] *Constitution of North Carolina,* art. IV, sec. 6.
[4] *Constitution of North Carolina,* art. IV, sec. 21.

matter of law or legal inference. And the jurisdiction of said court over "issues of fact" and "questions of fact" shall be the same as exercised by it before the adoption of the Constitution of one thousand eight hundred and sixty-eight and the Court shall have power to issue any remedial writs to give it a general supervision and control over the proceedings of the inferior courts.

Section 9 prescribes the original jurisdiction of the Supreme Court, but since this jurisdiction is limited to matters purely of a civil nature the section may be omitted from this discussion.

The terms of the Supreme Court are fixed by statute. There are to be two terms of the Court each year commencing on the first Monday in February and the last Monday in August. The Court is to sit at each term till all the business on the docket is determined or continued on good cause shown.[5]

The opinions and judgments of the Court are to be in writing, but the judges are not required to write their opinions in full except in cases in which they deem it necessary.[6]

Finally a statute provides that when an appeal is taken to the Supreme Court from any interlocutory judgment, the Supreme Court is not to enter any judgment, or order, or decree so appealed from but is to cause its opinion to be certified to the court below, with instructions to proceed upon such order, judgment, or decree, or to reverse or modify the same according to the opinion, and the court below is to enter upon its records the opinion at length and proceed in the cause according to instructions.[7]

[5] *Consolidated Statutes of North Carolina* (hereafter referred to as *Consolidated Statutes*), sec. 1408.   Raleigh, 1919.
[6] *Consolidated Statutes,* sec. 1416.
[7] *Ibid.,* sec. 1413.

SUPERIOR COURTS

The Constitution provides that "the State shall be divided into nine judicial districts, for each of which a judge shall be chosen; and there shall be held a Superior Court in each county at least twice in each year, to continue for such time as may be prescribed by law. But the General Assembly may reduce or increase the number of districts."[8] This number has been increased from time to time until by the statute of 1913 the number was increased to twenty.[9] By the Act of 1915, two judicial divisions, the Eastern and the Western, were created.[10]

The judges of the Superior Courts are elected in like manner as is provided for Justices of the Supreme Court, and they hold office for a term of eight years. It is also provided that the General Assembly may enact laws so that the judge shall be chosen from the district rather than by the voters of the whole State.[11] This of course has been done.

It is further provided by the Constitution[12] and by statute[13] that every judge of the Superior Court shall reside in the district for which he is elected, and that he shall preside in the courts of the different districts successively, but no judge shall hold court in the same district oftener than once in four years.

The jurisdiction of the courts inferior to the Supreme Court is vested by the Constitution in the Gen-

[8] *Constitution of North Carolina,* art. IV, sec. 10.
[9] *Public Laws of North Carolina, 1913,* c. 63; 1913, c. 196.
[10] *Ibid.,* 1915, c. 15.
[11] *Constitution of North Carolina,* art. IV, sec. 21.
[12] *Constitution of North Carolina,* art. IV, sec. 11.
[13] A. H. Mitchie, *Code of N. C.,* 1927, sec. 1446. Charlottesville, Va.

eral Assembly to be distributed among the several courts.[14] The following statute prescribes the original jurisdiction of the Superior Courts:

The Superior Court has original jurisdiction of all civil actions whereof exclusive original jurisdiction is not given to some other court; and of all criminal actions in which the punishment may exceed a fine of fifty dollars, or imprisonment for thirty days; and of all such affrays as shall be committed within one mile of the place where, and during the time, such court is being held; and of all offenses whereof exclusive original jurisdiction is given to a justice of the peace, if some justice of the peace shall not within twelve months after the commission of the offense proceed to take cognizance thereof.[15]

Concurrent and appellate jurisdiction is prescribed by the following statute:

In all cases in which by any statute original jurisdiction of criminal actions has been taken from the Superior Court and vested exclusively in the courts of inferior jurisdiction, such exclusive jurisdiction of such actions shall be concurrent and exercised by the court first taking cognizance thereof. Appeals shall be, as heretofore, to the Superior Court from all judgments of such inferior courts. . . .

In the case of *Rhyne* v. *Lipscombe,* 122 N. C. 650 (1898), there is a good discussion of the jurisdiction of the various courts inferior to the Supreme Court. It was held that in construing legislation establishing courts inferior to the Supreme Court and affecting the jurisdiction of the Superior Courts, the term "Superior Court" must be interpreted in the sense it had at the time of the adoption of the Constitution which established such court, which was that it was the highest court in the State next to the Supreme

[14] *Constitution of North Carolina,* art. IV, sec. 12.
[15] *Consolidated Statutes,* sec. 1436.

Court and superior to all others from which alone appeals lay direct to the Supreme Court, and possessed of general jurisdiction, criminal as well as civil, and both in law and equity.

In the same case it was further held that appeals from such courts, inferior to the Supreme Court, as the General Assembly may establish, lie (mediately or immediately as the General Assembly may prescribe) to the Superior Courts, and thence only to the Supreme Court.[16]

There seems to be no specific statute which would require that all appeals to the Supreme Court shall be from the Superior Court, but the above decision of the Court makes the point clear. Besides, there is a system of appeals provided from the other inferior courts to the Superior Court, and the only way of getting the case before the Supreme Court is through an appeal from the Superior Court. It is well that appeals lie only from the Superior Courts in this state for there are so many different kinds of recorders' courts that the Supreme Court docket would be badly crowded with cases that might very well be finally disposed of in the Superior Courts.

The Constitution provides[17] that a solicitor shall be elected from each judicial district, by the qualified voters thereof, as is prescribed for members of the General Assembly, who shall hold office for a term of four years, and prosecute on behalf of the state in all criminal actions in the Superior Courts, and advise the officers of justice in his district. Formerly the solicitor received a fee for each conviction, but this was unsatisfactory both from the viewpoint of the solicitor, where there was not much business, and it was also

[16] *Ibid.*, secs. 1437-1439.
[17] Art. IV, sec. 23.

unsatisfactory from the standpoint of the administration of justice because it sometimes led to persecution rather than prosecution in order to secure the fee. So in 1923, the Legislature passed a law placing solicitors on a salary of $4,500 per year.[18]

COURTS OF JUSTICES OF THE PEACE

The other courts specifically named in the Constitution are the Courts of Justices of the Peace. The *Consolidated Statutes,* Section 1463, provides that at every general election for members of the General Assembly three justices of the peace shall be elected in each township. In townships where an incorporated town is located, there is to be a justice of the peace for each one thousand inhabitants of such town. They are to hold office for a term of two years. Section 1468 of the *Consolidated Statutes* provides that the governor may at his discretion appoint one or more fit persons in every county to act as justices of the peace. The term of their office is four years from the date of their appointment.

The criminal jurisdiction of these courts is established by the State Constitution, Article IV, Section 27.

The several justices of the peace shall have jurisdiction, under such regulations as the General Assembly shall prescribe . . . of all criminal matters arising in their counties where the punishment cannot exceed a fine of fifty dollars or imprisonment for thirty days. . . . When an issue of fact shall be joined before a justice, on demand of either party thereto, he shall cause a jury of six men to be summoned, who shall try the same. . . . In all cases of a criminal nature the party against whom the judgment is given may appeal to the Superior Court, where the matter shall

[18] *Public Laws of North Carolina, 1923,* c. 157.

be heard anew. In all cases brought before a justice, he shall make a record of the proceedings, and file same with the clerk of the Superior Court for his county.

Consolidated Statutes, Section 1481, also provides that: justices of the peace shall have exclusive original jurisdiction of all assaults, assaults and batteries, and affrays, where no deadly weapon is used and no serious damage is done, and of all criminal matters arising in their counties, where the punishment prescribed by law does not exceed a fine of fifty dollars or imprisonment for thirty days: Provided, that justices of the peace shall have no jurisdiction over assaults with intent to kill, or assaults with intent to commit rape, except as committing magistrates: Provided further, that nothing in this section shall prevent the superior or criminal courts from finally hearing and determining such affrays as shall be committed within one mile of the place where and during the time such court is being held; nor shall this section be construed to prevent said courts from assuming jurisdiction of all offenses whereof exclusive original jurisdiction is given to justices of the peace, if some justice of the peace within twelve months after the commission of the offense, shall not have proceeded to take official cognizance of the same.

The courts of justices of the peace have a very limited final jurisdiction. But the work of these courts is important, particularly with regard to preliminary hearings. Regardless of the nature of the crime committed, the case may first be brought before a justice of the peace for preliminary hearing and for the determination of the bail bond for appearance before a court of higher jurisdiction. An indictment may be made by a grand jury, of course, in the Superior Court, but many of the graver crimes are first brought before a justice of the peace to prevent the escape of the accused party before the regular session of the Superior

Court convenes. Perhaps the finest work that the justices of the peace do toward the administration of criminal justice is to find out the facts, and if there is sufficient evidence bind the defendant over to the Superior Court or commit him to jail. In this way many criminals who would leave the jurisdiction before the meeting of the grand jury find themselves in the toils of the law by authority of the justice of the peace.

RECORDERS' COURTS

Besides the courts provided for in the Constitution a number of others have been created by statute. Prior to 1919, inferior courts had been created in different localities under different names with varying jurisdictions. These courts were created by special act of the Legislature and there is little uniformity in the system. The Act of 1919 made no attempt to reorganize these courts on a uniform basis, but it did create a sort of system for the future organization of such courts. Under this Act[19] provision is made for three kinds of courts: Municipal Recorders' Courts, County Recorders' Courts and Municipal-County Courts. These courts are all more or less alike in personnel, organization and jurisdiction.

The general law is optional and provides that the above courts may be established when so desired by the fulfillment of certain conditions stated in the statute as to population, etc.

In each of these courts there is to be a recorder elected by popular vote in the same manner as is provided for the election of other local officers. His salary is fixed in advance by the governing body of the town, city or county in which the court is to be established.[20]

[19] *Consolidated Statutes,* secs. 1536, 1563, 1583.
[20] *Consolidated Statutes,* secs. 1537, 1564, 1584.

The courts are to be open for the trial of criminal cases at least one day in each week and are to remain in session from day to day until all business is legally disposed of.[21]

The criminal jurisdiction of County Recorders' Court is set forth in the *Consolidated Statutes,* Section 1567. The jurisdiction of the other two courts is so similar to that set forth in this statute that it is unnecessary to quote the statutes prescribing their jurisdiction. The statue is as follows:

The court shall have jurisdiction in all criminal cases arising in the county which are now or may hereafter be given to a justice of the peace, and, in addition to the jurisdiction conferred by this section, shall have exclusive original jurisdiction of all other criminal offenses committed in the county below the grade of a felony as now defined by law, and the same are hereby declared to be petty misdemeanors: Provided, however, that where a special court or recorder's court shall legally exist within such county by virtue of a special act of the legislature passed before the amendments to the constitution in reference thereto, then the county recorder's court, as herein established, shall not have jurisdiction of criminal cases within the territory of such existing recorder's court, so as to interfere with or conflict with the existing recorder's court, but shall have concurrent jurisdiction where the jurisdiction of the two courts covers the same causes or the same subject-matter. This article and the establishment of any court thereunder shall not be construed to repeal, modify or in any wise affect any existing special court or recorder's court by virtue of such former special acts herein referred to.

It is further provided in Section 1586, *Consolidated Statutes,* that any recorder may sentence any person

[21] *Ibid.,* secs. 1538, 1565.

convicted of any offense punishable by imprisonment, to be imprisoned and worked on the local chain-gang, or such workhouse or other penal institutions, for such time as the recorder may in his discretion determine in accordance with the law.

There is to be a prosecuting attorney in each of these courts whose duty it is to appear in all prosecutions on behalf of the state. He may be elected or appointed to his office.[22]

It is also provided by statute that in all trials in the court, upon demand for a jury by the defendant or the prosecuting attorney that the recorder shall try the case in like manner as is provided in actions before justices of the peace wherein a jury is demanded, and that the same procedure as is provided by law for jury trials before justices of the peace shall apply.[23]

COUNTY COURTS

In 1923 an act was passed by the Legislature for the purpose of relieving congestion in court dockets and to provide needed facilities for speedy trials. The act provided for the establishment of general county courts. It is in the nature of a general law, and whether a county court shall be established in a particular county is left to the discretion of the county commissioners or the voters of the county. A detailed discussion of this court seems unnecessary since the organization and procedure is in most respects like that of the Superior Courts. The jurisdiction is practically the same in criminal cases as is provided for in the various Recorders' Courts of the state. Information is not at hand as to how many of these courts have been established. There is one in Forsyth County.

[22] *Consolidated Statutes,* secs. 1554, 1579.
[23] *Ibid.,* secs. 1555, 1572.

It is probable that more and more of these courts will be established as the dockets become congested and as needs arise. They may serve a very good purpose in relieving the Superior Courts of some of their burdens, but it seems that there are already too many different sorts of courts in the state. It is unfortunate that the system of inferior courts in the state was not planned but just happened in a haphazard fashion. There is great need for more uniformity in this matter. The only way uniformity can be secured now is to reorganize the whole system on a uniform basis. Whether this would be a wise thing to do is highly questionable.

STATUTES GOVERNING CRIMINAL PROCEDURE

The Code of Civil Procedure was adopted in North Carolina in 1868. It was taken over almost bodily from the state of New York and has been in general use ever since. But there is no code of criminal procedure in the state, many members of the bar to the contrary notwithstanding. In all the recent codifications of the laws there is a section devoted exclusively to criminal procedure. This section is now rather full and complete and covers most of the important phases of procedure in criminal cases, but in a strictly technical sense it cannot be called a code. Code procedure means that every step in the trial of the case is prescribed by the code and that common law has no application whatsoever in the process. North Carolina is a common-law state in criminal procedure, and, regardless of the large number of statutes that have been passed, common-law rules and principles are everywhere evident. There is much in the state criminal law and procedure that corresponds pretty closely to Book IV of Blackstone's *Commentaries*.

In a limited study of this kind it is unnecessary to trace the laws through their various codifications. Suffice it to say that the common law of England was transplanted into the colony of Carolina and that it has been developed and changed by statute from time to time to meet new conditions and new needs.

With each revision or codification of the general laws there has also been a collection and restatement of the statutes governing criminal procedure.

The more important of the compilations of the state statutes are: the *Revised Statutes of the State of North Carolina,* 1837,[24] prepared by Messrs. James Iredell and William H. Battle, 1837; the *Revised Code,* prepared by Messrs. B. F. Moore and Asa Biggs, 1855; the *Code,* prepared by Messrs. William T. Dortch, John Manning, and John S. Henderson, 1883; the *Revisal of 1905,* prepared by Messrs. Thomas B. Womack, Needham Y. Gulley and William B. Rodman; the *Revisal of 1908,* prepared by Mr. George P. Pell; *Consolidated Statutes,* prepared by Mr. L. P. McGehee, 1919, and the *North Carolina Code of 1927,* prepared by Mr. A. Hewson Michie. All of these compilations were adopted by the State Legislature except the *Revisal of 1908* and the *North Carolina Code of 1927.*

RULES GOVERNING APPEALS AND DISMISSALS

During this period (1890 to 1927) 2,183 criminal cases were taken to the Supreme Court either by ap-

[24] The Preface to the *Revised Statutes of the State of North Carolina, 1837,* prepared by Messrs. James Iredell and William H. Battle, contains a brief history of legislation in North Carolina from the "Grand Assembly of the County of Albemarle," 1666 or 1667, to the legislation which resulted in "Potter's Revisal," prepared in 1821.

peal or writ of certiorari. It is interesting to note that 341 cases were dismissed for the reason that the defendant had failed to perfect his appeal. The number of cases dismissed is surprisingly high in view of the apparently simple laws governing appeals in the state. But where there has been a non-compliance with the laws governing appeals or with the rules of the Court, dismissals have invariably followed as a result.

Rules of practice in the Supreme Court with amendments thereto, appear from time to time in the North Carolina *Reports*.[25] These rules are of necessity somewhat complex but certainly not more so than other legal forms and procedure. Rule 5, as to when actions are heard; Rule 6 as to criminal actions; and Rule 17 with regard to failure to docket in time, have been responsible for many dismissals. Rules 22, 23, and 24 with regard to printing the transcript have also proved fatal to many appeals.

In studying these criminal cases six tables have been prepared which throw some light on the number and character of the cases appealed, the grounds for the appeal and the action of the Court in affirming or reversing the decisions of the lower courts and the reasons for such action.[26] Table I shows the comparative number of cases appealed by the defendant and by the state with the action of the Supreme Court upon appeal by years and for the total period. Table II shows the total number of cases appealed by years and for the entire period with the action of the Supreme Court in affirming, reversing and remanding or reversing the case on appeal.   Table III contains a classification of the

[25] 115 N. C. Appendix (1894) ; 185 N. C. Appendix (1923) ; 192 N. C. Appendix (1926).

[26] See *infra*, pp. 23-33.

cases according to the nature of the crime committed with the action of the Supreme Court upon the cases. Table IV contains a classification of the cases appealed by the defendant according to the nature of the crime committed with the action of the Supreme Court upon the cases. Table V is similar to Table IV except that it shows the cases appealed by the state. Table VI contains the cases reversed and remanded or reversed by years and for the entire period with a classification according to the nature of the error committed by the lower court.

CHAPTER II

APPEAL BY THE STATE

THE RIGHT OF THE STATE TO APPEAL

THE RIGHT of the state to appeal has long been a moot question. Under the common law the state had no right of appeal in a criminal action, and the right is not generally considered as existing at the present time unless specifically authorized by statute. Practice in the United States is not uniform. Connecticut[1] apparently has almost an unlimited right of appeal while at the other extreme is Texas with no right of appeal under any circumstances. Practice in the other states varies between these two extremes. In North Carolina a law was passed in 1883 which gave the state the right of appeal upon a special verdict, upon a demurrer, upon a motion to quash, and upon arrest of judgment.[2] It should be noted that the right of the state to appeal is limited to points of law.[3]

In the early case of *State* v. *Lane,* 78 N. C. 547 (1878), Rodman, J. dismissing an appeal said:

[1] *Connecticut General Statutes,* 1918, sec. 6648.

[2] An appeal to the Supreme court may be taken by the state in the following cases, and in no other. Where judgment has been given for the defendant: 1. Upon a special verdict; 2. Upon a demurrer; 3. Upon a motion to quash; 4. Upon arrest of judgment.

[3] Since appeal by the state is limited to points of law only, the question of double jeopardy has not been seriously considered by the Court. As in the case of Connecticut there is no specific state constitutional provision prohibiting double jeopardy and of course the Fifth amendment to the Constitution of the United States is not binding upon the States in this matter. Perhaps this is one reason why double jeopardy has not been urged more strongly.

Until lately no case could be found in the English Reports, where a writ of error was allowed on behalf of the Crown in a criminal prosecution, and it has not yet been decided that such a writ may lawfully issue. . . .

From the cases there cited it will be seen that in many of the states it is held that the state has no right of appeal in a criminal case under any circumstances. In all, or nearly all, it seems to be held that where the right of appeal exists, it is given by statute; and if it exists at all independently of statute, it is confined to two cases only: One where the inferior court has given a judgment for the defendant and upon a demurrer to an indictment, or upon a motion to quash, which is considered as substantially similar.

In this State it has been recognized as existing in those two cases, but I am not aware that it has been in any others. Thus limited, the right may be defended by reasoning although not expressly given by any statute, it violates no principle and can never be used oppressively. Clearly in this State, an appeal by the State is not a general right, and if it is claimed in any case other than those mentioned the claim must be derived from some statute conferring it.

Thus the Supreme Court foreshadowed the law of 1883 which embodies two of the principles enunciated in the *Lane* case. This statute seems to have grown out of necessity. It is the result of both legislative and judicial experience. This right of appeal is very limited and the Court has construed the statute strictly, but it has resulted in a number of convictions where under the common-law rule the defendant would have been acquitted.

The Extent of State Appeal

It would be interesting to see how widely state appeal has been used since the passage of the law of 1883, but accurate information is wanting. With regard to the number of appeals dismissed the task seems hopeless, because, particularly in recent years, a list of cases has been given at the end of the *Reports* without any statement of whether the appeal was taken by the defendant or the state. The Attorney General's Report throws very little light on the matter as these cases are given with the simple statement "docketed and dismissed."

The following table, though inaccurate and incomplete, shows something of the comparative number of cases appealed by the defendant and the number appealed by the state, where the case was actually decided by the Supreme Court. It also shows, by years and for the total period, the number of cases affirmed, reversed and remanded and reversed. But there were 115 *per curiam* cases, or cases decided without a written opinion, in which it did not appear whether the defendant or the state was appellant. If these *per curiam* cases could be transferred to the columns where the appellant was known, it might change the percentages somewhat; but no doubt the 1,237 cases considered under the headings, "Appeal by Defendant," and "Appeal by the State," are sufficient to show the trends.

The table following shows that a total of 1,842 cases were decided by the Supreme Court from 1890 to 1927 inclusive. Appeal was taken by the defendant in 1,544 cases, or 83.7 per cent. Of this number 1,054 cases, or 68 per cent were affirmed on appeal, while 381 cases, or 24 per cent were reversed and remanded and 109, or 7 per cent were reversed. 183 cases, or nearly 10 per cent, were appealed by the state. Of this number eighty-eight cases, or 47 per cent, were affirmed while eighty-six cases, or 46 per cent, were reversed and remanded and nine cases, or 5 per cent, were reversed. Of the 115 *per curiam* cases where the appellant could

TABLE I[4]

YEAR	Appeal by Defendant				Appeal by State				Per Curiam			
	Aff.	R. & R.	Rev.	Total	Aff.	R. & R.	Rev.	Total	Aff.	R. & R.	Rev.	Total
1890	43	15	5	63	2	9		11				
1891	24	4	4	32	1	12		13				
1892	21	8	3	32	3	5		8				
1893	18	9	3	30	6	2		8				
1894	31	5	3	39	2	3		5				
1895	28	18	2	48	3	2		5				
1896	35	15	5	55	4			4		2		2
1897	37	15	2	54	4			4				
1898	15	9		24	1			1	4			4
1899	14	14	3	31	2	5		7	3	1		4
1900	25	7	7	39	3	3		6	9			9
1901	20	5	3	28	5	1	1	7	8			8
1902	13	16	5	34	4	3		7	6	3		9
1903	16	16	4	36	2	4	1	7	11	2		13
1904	12	17	3	32	2	1		3	7	1		8
1905	23	6	2	31	2	2		4	17			17
1906	24	6	3	33	1	2		3	16			16
1907	27	6	2	35	4	1		5				
1908	26	5	2	33	3	3	1	7	2			2
1909	28	14	4	46	3	3		6	4			4
1910	29	9	3	41	1			1				
1911	31	9	2	42	1	2		3	5			5
1912	27	1		28	3	3	1	7				
1913	25	13	4	42	2	1		3				
1914	38	7	2	47	2	2		4	1			1
1915	30	5	3	38	2	7	2	11	1			1
1916	24	5	3	32	1	2		3				
1917	18	5	1	24	3	1		4				
1918	26	5	3	34	1			1				
1919	34	8	1	43	1	2		3	4			4
1920	24	10	2	36	2			2				
1921	40	10	3	53	3	1		4				
1922	38	16	4	58	1			1				
1923	42	12	2	56	1	1		2			1	1
1924	47	9	2	58	1	1		2	3	3		6
1925	42	10	2	54	1			1				
1926	32	14	3	49	4	1		5				
1927	27	23	4	54	1	1	3	5		1		1
Total	1054	381	109	1544	88	86	9	183	101	13	1	115

[4] Some difficulty was experienced in preparing Table I. In

not be determined, 101 were affirmed, thirteen reversed and remanded, and one reversed outright. From the

theory it would seem an easy matter to read a case and decide whether it was affirmed, reversed and remanded, or reversed outright, but in reality the task is not so simple. In those cases where the judgment was affirmed the Court used the words "no error" or "affirmed." But in the cases not affirmed such words as "new trial," "venire de novo," "error," "judgment arrested," "reversed," "reversed and remanded," etc. were used. The words are more or less technical in their meaning and seem to have been used interchangeably at times by certain members of the Court.

The three rules of the Court are as follows: 1. In jury trials the result is "no error" or "new trial." 2. In equity cases and in cases involving the construction of deeds, contracts, etc., the result is "affirmed" or "error." 3. In cases pertaining only to questions of law, like motions to nonsuit, the result is "affirmed" or "reversed."

For the purpose of this study, technical distinctions may be disregarded as we are concerned only with distinguishing between those cases which have been reversed and remanded and those which have been reversed outright. Cases where a "new trial" was granted, a "venire de novo" awarded, or where the order was "reversed and remanded" have been placed under the heading of reversed and remanded. Where the lower court quashed the bill of indictment in the belief that it was defective, and the Supreme Court held the bill sufficient, etc., the cases have been placed under the reversed and remanded group. The cases where "judgment was arrested" on appeal, nothing else appearing, were placed under the group reversed outright. Some of the cases where the word "error" was used were also placed in this class as it was evident that the decision ended the case. The greater part of the cases where the word "reversed" was used were placed in this group; however, in a few cases it was evident that the case must go back for further proceedings and the cases were placed under the second group.

In discussing the tables and the cases we shall use the word reversed in its broad, general sense which includes both the cases reversed and remanded and those reversed. The real distinction between the two is not of very great importance in foregoing table it is obvious that most of the appeals to the Supreme Court are taken by the defendant, 83 per cent, as compared with 10 per cent by the state. It also appears that the percentage of affirmances is very much higher in the cases appealed by the defendant than by the state, the ratio being 68 per cent for the defendant and 47 per cent for the state. On appeal by the state 46 per cent were reversed and remanded while on defendant's appeal 24 per cent were reversed and remanded. The percentage of reversals was somewhat higher on the defendant's appeal than on the state's, the ratios being respectively 7 per cent and 5 per cent. With the limited information available in the table there are no outstanding tendencies apparent as to whether the state is using its right of appeal more or less as time goes on.

The Advantages of State Appeal

It can doubtless be said that this limited right of appeal by the state has done a great deal to facilitate the administration of criminal justice and to prevent guilty persons from escaping merited punishment. However, appeal by the state has advantages other than those just mentioned. Some trial judges have great fear of being reversed on appeal. Where the state has no right of appeal, there may be present the temptation to decide all close points of law in favor of the defendant in order to prevent his noting exceptions and taking an appeal. Under circumstances of this kind a ruling against the state right is always safe, for it is final and

most cases anyway. Judgment may be arrested in a case for a defective indictment but the prisoner may be held for a new bill, etc. A case may be reversed outright and still have to go back to the lower court for its final disposition.

no appeal lies regardless of the injustice of the point decided. Again, where the right of review is denied on the state's appeal, there is not only the possibility but the likelihood that there will be no uniformity in the various jurisdictions of the state as to what points should be decided in favor of the state and what points should be decided in favor of the defendant. In one district every point may be decided for the defendant to preclude the chances of appeal, while in an adjoining district a judge, who is more or less indifferent to appeal from his decisions, may decide the points raised in exactly the opposite manner. But only those cases where the defendant appeals could ever come before the Court for review and very little would be known as to what rulings the trial judges are making. Where appeal can be taken by the state as well as the defendant, nearly all the important rulings come before the Supreme Court and its decisions and opinions establish uniformity and serve as a criterion by which the lower courts may govern their conduct. Finally a good many cases are rather summarily dismissed by the trial judge (how many, cannot be determined without an examination of the court records in each judicial district). Sufficient information is not available at present to say that the judges have abused their discretion in dismissing cases, but no harm could result, and some good might be accomplished, if the right of the state to appeal were extended so as to cover cases of this kind.

CHAPTER III

TABULAR STATEMENT AND
EXPLANATIONS

TABLE I has already been discussed in connection with "Appeal by the State." Table II shows the total number of cases appealed to the Supreme Court for each of the thirty-eight years of the period. It shows the total number of cases affirmed by years and for the total period. It shows the number of cases reversed and remanded by years and for the whole period, and also the cases reversed outright by years and for the entire period.

Table III contains a classification of the cases as to the more important crimes involved for the total period (1890-1927). There were 1,051 cases miscellaneous in their nature. The majority of the cases in this group are misdemeanors; such as the violation of town and city ordinances, peddling goods without a license, selling liquor without a license, trespass, removal of crops, petty theft, injury to personal property, slander, abandonment, vagrancy, disorderly conduct, and the like. This classification also contains a few felony cases which do not properly come under any of the general divisions in the table.

The cases in Table III may be divided into three groups, those against the person, those against property, and those against public justice. Taking first the cases against the person, the percentage of affirmances was 67.7 per cent, and of the reversals, 32.3 per cent. This group includes murder, manslaughter, rape, carnal knowledge, assault with deadly weapons, and assault with intent to commit rape. In the cases against

TABLE II[1]

Year	Affirmed	Reversed and Remanded	Reversed	Total
1890.............	45	24	5	74
1891.............	25	16	4	45
1892.............	24	13	3	40
1893.............	24	11	3	38
1894.............	33	8	3	44
1895.............	31	20	2	53
1896.............	39	17	5	50
1897.............	41	15	2	58
1898.............	20	9		29
1899.............	19	20	3	42
1900.............	37	10	7	54
1901.............	33	6	3	42
1902.............	23	22	5	50
1903.............	29	22	5	56
1904.............	21	19	3	43
1905.............	42	8	2	52
1906.............	41	9	3	53
1907.............	31	7	2	40
1908.............	31	8	3	42
1909.............	35	17	4	56
1910.............	30	9	3	42
1911.............	37	11	2	50
1912.............	30	4	1	35
1913.............	27	11	4	45
1914.............	41	9	3	53
1915.............	33	12	5	50
1916.............	25	7	3	35
1917.............	21	5	1	27
1918.............	27	5	3	35
1919.............	39	10	1	50
1920.............	26	10	2	38
1921.............	43	11	3	57
1922.............	39	16	4	59
1923.............	43	13	3	59
1924.............	51	13	2	66
1925.............	43	10	2	55
1926.............	36	15	3	54
1927.............	28	25	7	60
Total.........	1243	480	119	1842

[1] There are a number of bastardy cases which have been omitted from the table. There was a time when a proceeding

Four-Year Moving Averages of the Cases in Table II Showing the Secular and Straight-Line Trends

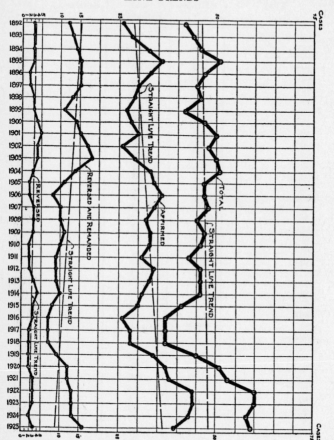

in bastardy was regarded as of a criminal nature, but it has been held in recent years that bastardy is a civil action.

To the above table might be added 23 *habeas corpus* cases but they will be considered separately. See *infra.*, p. 131.

property the affirmances were somewhat higher, being 71.5 per cent and the reversals, 28.5 per cent. In this list are arson, burglary, embezzlement, forgery, false pretense, larceny, highway robbery, or larceny from the person, and burning. The last class, public justice, includes perjury, bribery, official misconduct, compounding felonies, and the obstruction of justice. It is in this class that the percentage of affirmances is lowest, 49 per cent being affirmed and 51 per cent reversed.

TABLE III

Crime	Affirmed	Reversed and Remanded	Reversed	Total
Murder first.......	133	45	1	179[2]
Murder second.....	81	21		102
Manslaughter......	69	29	3	101
Arson.............	5	5		10
Burglary first......	8	1	1	10
Burglary second....	8			8
Rape.............	19	8	1	28
Carnal knowledge..	4	3		7
Embezzlement.....	13	9	2	24
Forgery...........	11	5		16
False pretense.....	17	10	6	33
Perjury...........	9	9	5	23
Larceny...........	57	33	2	92
Highway robbery or larceny from the person.......	9	5		14
Assault with deadly weapons..	51	29	4	84
Assault to rape.....	17	9		26
Burning...........	32	1	1	34
Miscellaneous......	700	257	94	1051
Total.........	1243	480	119	1842

[2] Before 1893 there were no degrees in murder and up to 1896 some cases were tried under the old law; so there may be a slight inaccuracy in the table with regard to the classification of murder in the first and second degrees.

Table IV is similar to Table III except that it shows the cases in which the defendant appealed, whereas Table III shows all the cases—those appealed by the defendant, by the state and the *per curiam* cases. The 1,051 cases headed "Miscellaneous" in Table III are omitted from Tables IV and V.

TABLE IV

Crime	Affirmed	Reversed and Remanded	Reversed	Total
Murder first.......	132	43	1	176
Murder second.....	81	21		102
Manslaughter......	69	29	3	101
Arson............	5	5		10
Burglary first......	8	1	1	10
Burglary second....	8			8
Rape.............	17	8	1	26
Carnal knowledge..	4	2		6
Embezzlement.....	12	7	2	21
Forgery...........	11	5		16
False Pretense.....	15	6	6	27
Perjury...........	8	7	4	19
Larceny...........	56	33	2	91
Highway robbery or larceny from the person.......	9	5		14
Assault with deadly weapons..	49	24	4	77
Assault to rape.....	17	8		25
Burning...........	32	1	1	34
Total.........	533	205	25	763

Table V is similar to Table IV except that it shows the cases in which the appeal was taken by the state. A comparison of Tables IV and V shows that the defendant appealed in 763 cases, or 96.5 per cent, and the state in twenty-eight cases, or 3.5 per cent. There were no *per curiam* cases in this group.

TABLE V

Crime	Affirmed	Reversed and Remanded	Reversed	Total
Murder first.......	1	2	..	3
Murder second.....	..	..	..	
Manslaughter......	..	..	..	
Arson.............	..	..	..	
Burglary first......	..	..	..	
Burglary second....	..	..	..	
Rape..............	2	..	..	2
Carnal knowledge..	..	1	..	1
Embezzlement.....	1	2	..	3
Forgery...........	..	..	..	
False pretense......	2	4	..	6
Perjury...........	1	2	1	4
Larceny...........	1	..	..	1
Highway robbery or larceny from the person.......	2	5	..	7
Assault with deadly weapons..	..	1	..	1
Assault to rape	..	..	..	
Burning...........	..	..	..	
Total.........	10	17	1	28

Table VI shows the number of cases reversed and remanded, or reversed by years and for the total period, with classification according to the sort of error committed.

Table VI is not satisfactory, nor is it what was originally planned in regard to showing the causes for reversal, but it seems to be the only practical method of tabular presentation. The original plan was to consider all the assignments of error in all the cases, those affirmed as well as those reversed, and see how the Court disposed of each exception. This course was followed in the preparation of some of the cases, but when as many as 178 exceptions were noted in the

TABLE VI

Year	Violation of Constitutional Provisions	Defective Indictments	Quashals	Variance between the Allegation and Proof	Instruction to the Jury	Evidence	Insufficient Evidence	Form of Verdict	Judgment on Special Verdict	Unconstitutional Ordinances or Laws	Jurisdiction	Misconduct of Court	Misconduct of Counsel	Miscellaneous	Total
1890	1	3	6		12	1	1	3						2	29
1891	1	4	6		1	1	1		4		1			1	20
1892	1	1	3	1	4	1			3			1		1	16
1893		1			5	2	1	2	1		1	1			14
1894	1	2	1		3		1		2	1					11
1895	1	1	1		9	5			1	1				3	22
1896	1	1			13	3	1		3						22
1897		1			9	3	1		3						17
1898					8									1	9
1899	2	1	2		7	3		2	1	1	1			3	23
1900	1	3	1	1	3	1	2		3	1				1	17
1901			1		5	1			1	1					9
1902	1		2		11		12		1						27
1903		4	1		8	6			5				1	2	27
1904	1				12	4			2		1			2	22
1905	1				5	1	1		2						10
1906		1	2	1	3	1	1		1		1			1	12
1907		2			3			2	1		1				9
1908			2		4				1	1	1	1		1	11
1909	1	3	2		5	4	1	1	1			1	1	1	21
1910		3			5	1	2						1		12
1911	2		1	2	4	2			1				1		13
1912			2		1				1				1		5
1913	1	1			11		1	1	1			1	1		18
1914		1			5	1		1	1		1	1		1	12
1915		1	3	1	4	1	1		3		1			2	17
1916				1	4	1	1	1	2						10
1917	1				1	1	1		1					1	6
1918		1			5	1							1		8
1919					7	1			1		1			1	11
1920	1			1	6	1			1		1			1	12
1921		1			6	3	2					1		1	14
1922	1		1		6	6		1	1		1		1	2	20
1923		1	1		6	4	1	1	1				1		16
1924				1	8	1	1		1					3	15
1925	1				7	1	1				1		1		12
1926	1	1			5	5	2		1				1	2	18
1927		1	1	1	10	9	1	1	3					5	32
Total	22	41	40	8	231	76	30	19	47	14	10	5	8	48	599

brief it became clear that such a treatment of the cases would not lend itself to statistical study. In most cases, where so many exceptions were taken the Court silently passed over them and reversed upon one or two main grounds or affirmed the case. Out of the abundance of caution, the counsel for the defendant must note every single exception which he uses or expects to use in his oral argument before the Court, since the Court will not hear arguments upon exceptions not noted in the brief. But in the consideration of the case, if the Court finds one reversible error the case will be reversed. As a rule the other assignments of error are not discussed at length in the opinion but rather summarily dismissed, unless there is a possibility that the case may again come before the Court, in which event the exceptions are disposed of in no doubtful manner. In a great many of the cases the Court makes it clear that the reversal was on one ground only. In others two or more points seem to be considered with about equal force. In a few cases it was necessary to choose between two or more reversible errors the one that seemed to influence the Court most, but a careful reading of the case and the head notes usually leaves little doubt as to the real cause of reversal.

Table VI shows that twenty-two cases were reversed because of the violation of some constitutional provision. A number of cases were reversed and remanded or simply remanded for proper sentence where the sentence of the court was inconsistent with the penalty provided in the statute. These cases were included in the miscellaneous group as they are violative of a statute rather than the Constitution. Forty-one cases were reversed because of defective indictments, and forty because of quashal in the lower courts or an arrest of judgment for a defective indictment. There were 231 reversals on account of improper instructions to the jury or the refusal of the trial judge to give proper instructions when requested to do so. Seventy-six cases were reversed on account of evidence, either because of the admission of improper evidence or the exclusion of evidence which should have been admitted. For variance between the allegation and the proof nine cases were reversed. Eight cases were reversed because of misconduct of the solicitor or counsel, and five because of misconduct of the court itself. Defective verdicts or an error in the form of the verdict was responsible for nineteen reversals. According to the table, only thirty cases were reversed on account of insufficient evidence, though in reality the number is somewhat larger. Often there was a reversal because the court refused to instruct the jury that there was not sufficient evidence to convict. In such instances the cases have been included under instruction to the jury, which of course is technically correct, though the case might just as well have been placed under the heading of insufficient evidence. There were fourteen reversals because the defendant had been convicted of the violation of a city ordinance or law which was unconstitutional or otherwise invalid. Forty-seven cases were reversed because of judgment on special verdict, ten because of lack of jurisdiction, and forty-eight for miscellaneous reasons. Under the head of miscellaneous comes a group of cases that cannot very well be placed in any of the other classes.

A more detailed consideration of Table VI seems necessary with regard to the main causes for the reversal of cases on appeal. This will require a study of some of the individual cases as decided by the Court. In this case study we shall be particularly concerned with the nature of the cases, the attitude of the Court, and the significant tendencies in the decisions and opinions of the Court.

CHAPTER IV

VIOLATION OF CONSTITUTIONAL PROVISIONS

THE PROVISIONS of the State Constitution with regard to the rights of the accused are contained in the *Declaration of Rights,* Article I, Sections 11-19 and 35.[1] The

[1] Sec. 11. In all criminal prosecutions every man has the right to be informed of the accusation against him and to confront the accusers and witnesses with other testimony, and to have counsel for his defense, and not be compelled to give evidence against himself, or to pay costs, jail fees, or necessary witness fees of the defense, unless found guilty.

Sec. 12. No person shall be put to answer any criminal charge, except as hereinafter allowed, but by indictment, presentment or impeachment.

Sec. 13. No person shall be convicted of any crime but by the unanimous verdict of a jury of good and lawful men in open court. The Legislature may however provide other means of trial for petty misdemeanors, with the right of appeal.

Sec. 14. Excessive bail shall not be required nor excessive fines imposed, nor cruel or unusual punishment inflicted.

Sec. 15. General warrants, whereby any officer or messenger may be commanded to search a suspected place, without evidence of the act committed, particularly described and supported by the evidence, are dangerous to liberty and ought not to be granted.

Sec. 16. There shall be no imprisonment for debt in this state, except in case of fraud.

Sec. 17. No person ought to be taken, imprisoned, or disseized of his freehold, liberties, or outlawed or exiled or in any manner deprived of his life, liberty or property, but by the law of the land.

Sec. 18. Every person restrained of his liberty is entitled to a remedy to enquire into the lawfulness thereof, and to remove the same if unlawful; and such remedy ought not to be delayed or denied.

Sec. 35. All courts shall be open; and every person for in-sections most often before the courts have had to do with juries, former conviction or acquittal, self-incriminating testimony, presence in open court, cruel and unusual punishments.

As already pointed out twenty-two cases were reversed because of the violation of some provision of the State or Federal Constitution. There were other cases in which a violation of constitutional rights was urged as a reason for reversal, and these doubtless played a part in influencing the Court, but the decision was primarily placed on some other ground. Cases involving admissions and confessions might be placed in this classification, but they will be considered under the heading of "Evidence." In a few cases defendant demanded a jury trial in petty misdemeanors, but since the constitution gives the legislature the control over such matters it is purely statutory.

THE JURY

In an unbroken line of decisions the Supreme Court has held that in all felony cases there must be a unanimous decision of a jury of twelve men to render a legal verdict.[2] While the Constitution does not state that there shall be a jury of twelve men, the Court has consistently held that at the time when the State Constitution was adopted a common-law jury of twelve men was contemplated.

In *State* v. *Baker,* 107 N. C. 913 (1890), defendant was convicted of perjury in the lower court. On appeal to the

jury done him in his lands, goods, person, or reputation, shall have remedy by due course of law, and rights and justice administered without sale, denial or delay.

[2] *State v. Scruggs,* 115 N. C. 805 (1894) ; *State v. Pulliam,* 184 N. C. 681 (1922) ; *State v. Hartsfield,* 188 N. C. 357 (1924) ; *State v. Berry,* 190 N. C. 363 (1925).

Supreme Court it was shown that only eleven men were present on the grand jury when the indictment was found. The Court held that a grand jury had a well-understood meaning at the adoption of our Declaration of Rights, and one of its most essential features was that the concurrence of twelve of its members was necessary to the finding of a presentment or indictment.

In this same case a law passed by the Legislature making the concurrence of nine members of a grand jury sufficient to finding an indictment was held unconstitutional.

In *State* v. *Rogers,* 162 N. C. 656 (1913), defendant was on trial for murder. One of the jurors was taken ill, and the trial proceeded with eleven jurors. There was a conviction of manslaughter. Upon appeal to the Supreme Court a new trial was ordered as eleven men were held not to constitute a lawful jury in felony cases and that the defendant himself did not have the right to waive the jury right in a case of this sort.

In *State* v. *Rouse,* 194 N. C. 318 (1927), the Rogers case was cited with approval by the Court in holding invalid a conviction by a jury of eleven men in a felony case. While taking evidence, one of the jurors was taken very ill. By agreement of counsel for the defendant, in the presence of the defendant, and of the Solicitor for the State, the juror was excused and the case completed with eleven jurors. On appeal the Court declared the verdict was a nullity and ordered a new trial.

In *State* v. *Wheeler,* 185 N. C. 670 (1923), the Court held that in trials for misdemeanors the defendant might consent to the trial of his case with a jury of eleven men when one was rendered incapable of service, though the case was decided on other grounds.

FORMER CONVICTION OR ACQUITTAL

The cases involving former conviction and acquittal as a bar to further prosecution were placed under the

"Violation of Constitutional Provisions" in the table. But as a matter of fact the Constitution has nothing to say on this point. Scant mention is made of it in the laws with regard to accessories before and after the fact in felonies, and also with regard to false pretenses and cheats.[3] The Federal Constitution does provide that "No person shall be . . . subject, for the same offense, to be twice put in jeopardy of life or limb." But this provision does not bind the states.[4] Yet from the earliest times our State Supreme Court has held that former acquittal or conviction is a bar to further proceedings. It is a maxim of common law that no person shall be twice placed in jeopardy for the same offense, and this principle is as thoroughly established as any provision of the State Constitution.

In *State* v. *Price,* 111 N. C. 703 (1892), assault and battery being charged, defendant was convicted in the court below but the Supreme Court reversed the decision on account of former acquittal.

In *State* v. *Reid,* 115 N. C. 741 (1894), the Supreme Court reversing a lower court held that a prosecution for selling liquor without a license, contrary to a city ordinance, is no bar to a prosecution by the State for the same act of selling without obtaining a State license.

In *State* v. *Fagg,* 125 N. C. 609 (1899), in an indictment for an affray where defendant had been convicted in a Justice's Court for participating in an affray, in which a deadly weapon was used, but not by him, it was held that his plea of *former conviction,* when indicted in the Superior Court for the same offense ought to have been sustained.

In *State* v. *Taylor,* 133 N. C. 755 (1903), defendant was indicted for assault with a deadly weapon. He claimed no deadly weapon was used and pleaded former conviction in

[3] *Consolidated Statutes,* secs. 4175, 4277.
[4] *Constitution of the United States,* Fifth Amendment.

the Mayor's Court. From a judgment for defendant the
State appealed. In reversing the decision it was held that
a conviction of violating a city ordinance punishing the
disturbance of the good order and quiet of the town was
not a bar to the prosecution by the State for an assault.

In *State* v. *Cale,* 150 N. C. 805 (1909), a trial before a
magistrate was upheld as a bar to further prosecution in
the Superior Court for the same offense.

Where a person has been convicted or acquitted on
a charge, the Supreme Court has consistently held that
he cannot again be tried for the same offense. On the
other hand, it has held that a conviction under a particular ordinance or law is not a bar to further prosecution for the violation of another ordinance or law.
A prosecution in one jurisdiction may or may not be
a bar to a prosecution in another, depending on the
jurisdiction of the courts and the identity of the offense
charged.

ABSENCE OF THE DEFENDANT FROM THE COURTROOM

A few cases have been reversed because the defendant
was not present when the sentence was pronounced or
because the conviction was not in open court, as required
by Section 13 of the *Declaration of Rights, supra,* p.
36. The following cases show something of the attitude
of the Court on these points:

In *State* v. *Cherry,* 154 N. C. 624 (1911), defendants
were on trial for larceny. During the process of the trial
they escaped but the court proceeded with the trial and
sentenced them to work on the roads. Later the defendants
were apprehended and appealed to the Supreme Court on
the ground that they were not present at the trial. It was
held that a sentence to work on the roads involved and included corporal punishment and that the defendant must be

present when sentence was pronounced in order for it to be valid, so a new trial was awarded.

In *State* v. *Pierce,* 123 N. C. 745 (1911), defendant was convicted of burning a gin house. He absented himself from the courtroom during the argument of his counsel, who waived the objection and proceeded with the argument. On appeal to the Supreme Court it was held that such absence was no ground for an exception in a case not capital.

The law seems to be that the prisoner has a right to be present during his trial upon the trial of a felonious offense not capital, but there is no principle, statute or precedent that makes it essential that he shall be. However, if the accused is temporarily and voluntarily absent, and especially if he flees from the court, such absence may be treated as a waiver of his right to be present during the trial. On the other hand, a judgment cannot be given against a person in his absence involving corporal punishment. He must be present when it is done. The prisoner must be present, of course, in the trial of a capital felony, and he cannot waive his right.

CRUEL OR UNUSUAL PUNISHMENT

Where it has been clearly shown that the sentence imposed upon a person accused of crime was cruel or unusual, the Court has consistently set the judgment aside or remanded the case for a proper sentence, for example:

In *State* v. *Smith,* 174 N. C. 804 (1917), defendant was charged with secret assault and convicted of assault with a deadly weapon or aggravated assault with a deadly weapon. The court sentenced the defendant to four years confinement in the penitentiary. On appeal to the Supreme Court, the judgment was set aside as being in contravention of Art. 1, Sec. 14, of the State Constitution.

Where the sentence has not been cruel or unusual, the decisions of the lower courts have not been disturbed as a general rule.

In *State* v. *Hatley,* 110 N. C. 522 (1892), defendants were convicted of keeping a disorderly house and were adjudged to be imprisoned and pay the costs. But the court at the same time directed that if the defendants left the State within thirty days, no *capias* was to be issued; defendants did leave, but returned into the State very soon afterwards, when they were arrested and imprisoned. On appeal to the Supreme Court it was held that while the court had no power to banish the defendants, the judgment in respect to imprisonment and costs was valid, and could be enforced upon their return to the State.

In *State* v. *Apple,* 121 N. C. 584 (1897), defendant was convicted in the lower court for assault combined with robbery. On appeal the Supreme Court held that a sentence of two years imprisonment and working on the roads was not cruel and unusual punishment for an unjustifiable and outrageous assault combined with robbery.

Considering the number of cases involving constitutional points, the reversals have been few indeed. We may be reasonably sure that one or two reversals grew out of an appeal to the Superior Court from that of a Justice of the Peace, where a bill of indictment was required but the matter was probably overlooked. The *Baker* case (see *supra,* p. 37) was undoubtedly decided as a result of the Legislature's making the finding of an indictment by nine grand jurors valid. One or two of the cases of former conviction or acquittal, as a bar to further prosecution, turned on a technicality of jurisdiction.

CHAPTER V

DEFECTIVE INDICTMENTS

EARLY HISTORY AND DEVELOPMENT OF INDICTMENTS

WHILE THIS study is confined to the period since 1890, it will be necessary to consider the early history and development of indictments in this state in order to explain present-day practices and tendencies of the courts with regard to this important matter. Our system of indictments has its roots and origin in the English law, and it will be helpful to take a look at some of the early English statutes both for the sake of comparison and for the explanation of our own procedure. It is in the matter of indictments that legal technicalities and absurdities are most conspicuous. It is here that the courts have been most sharply and severely criticised, and it is for this reason that a good deal of space will be given to the English background and the early period in this state.

Without going into the practice of the colonial period it is sufficient to say that the first state Constitution, that of 1776, required that an indictment, to be valid, must conclude "against the peace and dignity of the state."[1] This section, however, was omitted from the *Constitution of 1868.*

Martin, in his *Collection of the Statutes of the Parliament of England in Force in the State of North Carolina* (1792), gives the statute of 37 Henry VIII. We quote the entire statute as it throws much light on indictments in England, and besides it foreshadows important later statutes.

[1] *Constitution of 1776,* sec. 36.

The act of Vi & Armis *left out of any indictment lacking these words,* Vi & Armis, shall be good. Where before this time it was, and yet is commonly used in all indictments and inquisitions of treason, murder, felony and divers other, to have comprised and put in every the same indictments and inquisitions these words, *Vi et Armis,* and in divers of the same indictments to declare the manner of the force and arms; that is to say, Vi & Armis, videlicet, baculis, cultellis, arcubus & sagittis, or other such like words in effect, where of truth the parties so indicted had no manner of such weapons at the time of the said offense, committed and done; yet in default and lack of the same words, the said indictments were, and yet be, taken as void in law, for to put any person to answer thereunto; and the party or parties so indicted, for lack of the same words, not being comprised, and put in the said indictments by writ or writs of error, or by plea upon his or their appearance, as the same case did require; For reformation whereof, be it enacted by the King, our Sovereign lord, with the assent of, the lords, spiritual and temporal and of the commons, in this present Parliament assembled, and by the authority of the same THAT, from the feast of the Nativity of Our Lord God, next coming, these words VI & Armis, viz. cum baculis, cutellis, arcubus and sagattis, or such other like words, shall not of necessity be put or comprised in any inquisition or indictment, etc.[2]

A review of Martin's *Collection of Statutes* shows that the statute of jeofails was in force in the state in various forms and jurisdictions and was a well established principle of law in 1792. Chapter IV empowers justices to amend defaults in the records or processes before judgment is given. Chapter VI provides for the

[2] F. X. Martin, *A Collection of the Statutes of the Parliament of England in Force in the State of North Carolina,* chap. VIII, p. 256 (Newbern, 1792).

amendment of a record that is defective by misprision of the clerk. Chapter VII is an act to prevent arrests of judgment, and suspending executions. Chapter XII deals with what defects in records may be amended by judges, and what not and also states that no judgment or record shall be reversed for any writ, process, etc. raised. Chapter XIII sets forth an act for the further reformation of jeofails. Chapter XXX is devoted to mispleadings and jeofails. It has been a generally accepted principle in our jurisprudence that where a particular offense or method of procedure is not covered by statute the common law is to prevail. Considering the extent to which the English statutes and common law were in force in 1792 in this state, and considering the comparatively small number of statutes that have been enacted since that time, it is obvious that we are greatly beholden to the English system.

But regardless of the apparently liberal amendatory laws of the time concerning indictments they seem to have been little used and completely ignored by the Court, in some cases at least. We give the following case rather fully because it illustrates extreme technicality—happily not common. The long technical bill of indictment is given in full in order that it may be compared with some of the simpler forms of the present day. The reasoning of the Court is interesting, too, in that the judge seemed to be securely bound by the fetters of technicality. The dissenting opinion in the case shows a tendency to break away from mere form and over-refinement and to give the law a more practical application.

State v. *Carter,* 1 N. C. 319 (1801). This was an indictment against James Carter for the murder of William

Loaper, upon the bill in the words and figures following, to-wit:

State of North Carolina,
District of Fayetteville,
Superior Court of Law, April Term, 1801.

The jurors for the state upon their oaths, present, that James Carter, late of the county of Robinson, within the district aforesaid, labourer, not having the fear of God before his eyes, but being moved and seduced by the instigation of the devil, on the twenty-second day of November, in the year of our Lord, one thousand eight hundred, and in the XXVth year of the independence of the State, with force and arms, in the county aforesaid, in and upon one William Loaper, in the peace of God and the State, then and there being feloniously, wilfully, and with malice aforethought, did make an assault; and that he the said James Carter, with a certain knife of the value of sixpence, which he the said James Carter in his right hand then and there held, the said William Loaper, then and there in and upon the left breast of him the said William Loaper then and there feloniously, wilfully, and of his malice aforethought, did strike and thrust, thereby giving to the said William Loaper, then and there, with the knife aforesaid, in and upon the aforesaid left *brest* of him the said William Loaper, one mortal wound, of the breadth of one inch, and of the depth of four inches, of which said mortal wound the aforesaid William Loaper then and there instantly died; and so the jurors aforesaid, upon their oath aforesaid, do say that the said James Carter, the said William Loaper, in the manner aforesaid, feloniously, wilfully, and of his malice aforethought, did kill and murder, against the peace and dignity of the State.

Plea of not guilty—. The jury sworn to try the issue of traverse, found the prisoner guilty of the felony and murder, in the manner and form as charged in the bill of indictment. Counsel for the prisoner moved an arrest of judgment for the following reasons:

1. Because in the caption of the indictment, the term of the court is not sufficiently expressed, the year being written in numerical figures.

2. Because the place of the wound in that part of the indictment which charges with giving a mortal wound, and which states the length and breadth of the wound, is not sufficiently or at all set forth.

Johnston, J. I am of the opinion that the judgment should be arrested for the second reason, notwithstanding the meaning of the word *brest* is unequivocally explained by the antecedent words, where the wound is charged to be given under the left *breast,* and the mortal wound is charged to be given on "the aforesaid left *brest"; yet I consider myself bound by all the authorities which require the greatest strictness and accuracy in all capital proceedings, and which do not appear in any instance to have been dispensed with, though in some cases carried to a degree of critical exactness, not easily to be reconciled to good sense or sound understanding; and though this case may by some be considered of that description, yet I am not disposed to give a judgment which might appear in any respect to run counter to the opinion of the most learned and respectable judges, who have written or decided in like cases.

Hall and Macay, Judges agreed in opinion with Judge Johnston and the Judgment Arrested.

Taylor, J. dissented in this case, saying in part that he had no disposition to withhold his assent from the principle that a criminal charge, and particularly one which might affect the life of a citizen, should be expressed fully, clearly and accurately. A due observance of this principle guards against evils of discretional judicature; and while it affords additional security to civil freedom, and advances the claims of humanity, connects with the specific crime its legal and appropriate punishment. Wherever plain and intelligent authorities give countenance to an exception, either by application or just analogous reasoning—wherever the reason of the law speaks, though the law itself be silent, it is fit that objections so supported should be sustained by a court of justice. But according to my apprehension, the doctrine has already been extended to a sufficient degree, to answer all the purposes of security and justice; and to extend it further might justify those objections which have heretofore been alleged in reproach of the law.[3]

In sharp contrast with the *Carter* case is *State* v. *Owen*, 5 Murphey 452 (1810), the charge being murder. It is held that an indictment charging that A. B. with a certain stick, etc., in and upon the face of C. D. then and there feloniously, etc., did strike and beat, giving to the said C. D., then and there with the stick aforesaid, in and upon the head and face of the said C. D., several mortal wounds of which said several mortal wounds the said C. D. instantly died, is good; for there is in the first clause a direct allegation of a stroke, and the participle "giving" and the words "then and there" connect this allegation with the mortal wounds in the second clause. The struggle of the Court to break away from the purely technical point of view is well expressed by Taylor, J., in delivering the opinion of the Court in this case:

Like any other citizen in his situation, he is entitled to the full benefit of the constitutional provisions devised to promote the security of all; and though the most atrocious criminality may have been proved to the satisfaction of the jury, yet legal condemnation ought never to be separated from legal proofs. And we cannot too strongly impress it on our minds that want of requisite precision and certainty, which may at one time, postpone or ward off

[3] This case was decided by the Court of Conference which was the highest appellate court in the state at the time. See *supra* p. 5 for description of the Court of Conference.

the punishment of guilt, may, at another, present itself as the last hope and only asylum of persecuted innocence. It must, however, be confessed that this is, on the ancient reasoning on this branch of the law, a degree of the metaphysical and frivolous subtilty strongly characteristic of the age in which it was introduced, when at the revival of letters the first efforts of learning were laborious and rude, and scarcely a ray of common sense penetrated the clouds of pedantry. Were a system now to be established, it is probable that much of the jargon of the law would be exploded, and that no objection would prevail against an indictment, or any other instrument, which conveyed to the mind, in an intelligible form its intended impression. But we must follow in the footsteps of those who have preceded us until the Legislature thinks fit to interfere; though we have no wish to extend the particularity further.

While we are not prepared to assert that the statute of 1811 concerning indictments is the direct result of decisions of the Court, it does seem highly probable that the Legislature might have been influenced by such absurdities as the *Carter* decision and such constructive suggestions as appear in the *Owen* case. We are bound to recognize the constructive and progressive work of the Court in instances like the *Owen* case. Handicapped by the traditions and technicalities of common law, and without the aid of statutes, it pointed out many absurdities of the law and did much to blaze the way to more sane and simple forms of indictments.

As early as 1811 the Legislature passed an important statute with regard to indictments.[4] There can be no

[4] Every criminal proceeding by warrant, indictment, information, or impeachment shall be sufficient in form for all intents and purposes, if it expresses the charge against the defendant in a plain, intelligible, and explicit manner; and the same shall not be quashed nor the judgment thereon stayed, by reason

doubt as to its origin since 37 Henry VIII, with regard to abolishing "force and arms" in indictments, is specifically referred to (see *supra,* p. 44). But the statute goes further than the English one and declares that in all criminal proceedings the indictment shall be sufficient for all intents and purposes if it expresses the charge against the defendant in a plain, intelligible and explicit manner. It further provides that an indictment shall not be quashed or judgment stayed on account of any informality or refinement if sufficient matter appears in the bill to proceed to judgment. This statute is an important milestone in the administration of criminal justice. An appraisal of the value of this statute is perhaps best expressed by the Court itself and we shall give a few of its quotations.

Chief Justice Ruffin in the *Moses* case[5] said (referring to the statute of 1811), "this law was certainly designed to uphold the execution of public justice by freeing the courts from the fetters of form, technicality and refinement, which do not concern the substance of the charge and the proof to support it." Mr. Justice Ashe said in the *Parker* case, "ever since 1811 it has been the evident tendency of our courts as well as of our law-makers to strip criminal actions of the many refinements and useless technicalities with which they have been fettered by common law, the adherence to which often resulted in the obstruction of justice and the escape of malefactors from merited punishment."[6] Clark, J., in the *Barnes* case said, "The act has re-

of any formality or refinement, if in the bill or proceeding sufficient matter appears to enable the court to proceed to judgment.

[5] *State* v. *Moses,* 2 Dev. 452 (1830).

[6] *State* v. *Parker,* 81 N. C. 531 (1830).

ceived a very liberal construction and its efficacy has reached and healed numerous defects in the substance as well as in the form of indictments. . . . It is evident that the courts have looked with no favor on technical objections, and the legislature has been moving in the same direction. The current is all one way, sweeping off by degrees informalities and refinements, until indeed a plain, intelligible and explicit charge is all that is now required."[7]

Thus we see that the statute of jeofails is well established in our criminal procedure by legislative act and approved by judicial sanction. Though the statute is seldom referred to explicitly, its principles have a general application in North Carolina procedure.

IMPORTANT DECISIONS BASED ON TECHNICALITIES

Despite the law of 1811, and despite judicial utterances that the courts have looked with no favor on technical objections, many important decisions have turned on a mere technicality rather than on common sense. Some of the technicalities have grown out of the common law, for every indictment is presumed to be founded on the common law unless some statute is indicated by the drawer of the bill, on which he means to prosecute it. It seems that the court has experienced much difficulty in purging indictments of technicalities and in breaking away from the traditions and practices of common-law rules. The following cases are illustrative of this point:

In *State* v. *Jim,* 3 Murphey 1 (1819), a negro slave was indicted for breaking into a dwelling house with intent to steal a bank note. The indictment concluded, "contrary to

[7] *State* v. *Barnes,* 122 N. C. 1031 (1897).

the form of the *statute* in such cases made and provided."
At that time there appeared to be two statutes regulating
the larceny of bank notes. The bill was, therefore, quashed
and a new trial granted because it concluded in the singular,
"contrary to the form of statute" in such cases made and
provided, instead of the plural "contrary to the form of
statutes," in such cases made and provided. The judgment
of the lower court was reversed and the Court said "that
an innocent man might be surprised into conviction because
while he was preparing his defense under one statute the
prosecution might be arranging the charge under another,
etc."

In *State* v. *Sandy,* 3 Ired. 570 (1843), defendant was convicted of burning a storehouse. On appeal the Court held
that the bill of indictment was defective because there was
only one *statute,* and the bill of indictment concluded
against the form of the *statutes* and so judgment was arrested.

In *State* v. *Jesse,* 19 N. C. 298 (1837), it was held that
an indictment under the act of 1823 (Taylor's Revisal, Ch.
(1229) making an assault by a person of color upon a white
female with intent to commit a rape, capital, must charge
the assault to have been felonious; charging an assault,
with intent "feloniously to ravish," is not sufficient.

In *State* v. *Shaw,* 3 Ired. 20 (1842), defendant was tried
and convicted of refusing to assist an officer in securing a
person whom he had arrested. On appeal a new trial was
granted on the ground that it was not sufficient to state in
the indictment that this was an arrest by *lawful* authority
but that the authority to arrest must be set forth in the indictment.

In *State* v. *Fisher,* 25 N. C. 111 (1843), a defendant was
convicted in the lower court for disturbing a religious assembly, commonly called a "quarterly meeting conference."
On appeal the Court refused to sustain the indictment and
suggested that the bill should have stated that the assembly

had met for "divine worship," "divine service," "religious worship or service," or something of the same import.

In the above group of cases it seems that the bill of indictment in each case was sufficient to enable the court to proceed to judgment. From a study of later cases we have the feeling that if these cases were now presented to the Supreme Court the bill of indictment would be sustained as sufficient in every case.

DIVESTING INDICTMENTS OF SUPERFICIALITIES

Perhaps the best way to follow the positive work of the Court in divesting indictments of superficialities is to consider a number of cases in more or less detail.

In *State* v. *Sutton,* 5 Murphey 281 (1809), defendant, being convicted upon an indictment for riot, appealed to the Supreme Court. Judgment was arrested because the caption of the indictment did not describe the court before which it was found.

But in *State* v. *Brickell,* 1 Hawks 354 (1821), in an assault and battery case, the Court held that the caption of an indictment formed no part of it, and therefore it was not ground for arresting judgment, thus overruling the Sutton case.

In *State* v. *Moses,* 2 Dev. 452 (1830), the Court sustaining an indictment, held that by the act of 1811 all defects in indictments were cured, except the omission of an averment of facts and circumstances which constitute the crime charged. Nothing need be stated of which proof is not required on the trial. Therefore in an indictment for murder it is necessary to aver that the mortal wound was given, but the size and nature of the wound being matters not material to the description of the offense, nor a necessary part of the evidence, its dimensions need not be stated. In the same case an indictment concluding "and the jurors" omitting the word "so" was held sufficient.

In *State* v. *Joyner,* 81 N. C. 534 (1879), it was held that an indictment whether for a common law or statutory offense which does not conclude against the "peace and dignity of the state" was fatally defective.

But in *State* v. *Kirkman,* 104 N. C. 911 (1889), the *Joyner* case was definitely overruled and a formal conclusion was declared nonessential.

In an indictment under the act of 1830, Ch. 10, against a white man, for playing cards with slaves, it was held to be sufficient to charge, that the defendant "unlawfully did play at a game of cards," without specifying the name of the particular game played at with the cards.[8]

Upon a charge for fornication and adultery the Court sustained the indictment and said, "an indictment ought to be certain to every intent and without any intendment to the contrary. But if the sense be clear and the charge sufficiently explicit to support itself, nice objections ought not to be regarded."[9]

On a trial for murder the omission of *North Carolina* in an indictment found in a court of this state, where the name of the county is inserted in the margin or body of the indictment, was not a cause for arresting judgment.[10]

Where the indictment set forth the time of the commission of the murder, in these words: "On the third day of August, eighteen hundred and forty-three," without saying "the year of our Lord," or even using the word "year"; it was held that although this defect would have been fatal at common law, yet it is cured by our act of Assembly 1811.[11]

In the *Godet* case the defendant was indicted for stealing "a hog." The evidence showed that the animal was a shoat, between five and six months old. The Court held that an

[8] *State* v. *Ritchie* 2 D. & B. 29 (1836).
[9] *State* v. *Fore and Chestnut,* 23 Ired. 378 (1841).
[10] *State* v. *Lane,* 26 Ired. 113 (1843).
[11] *Ibid.*

indictment for stealing a hog is well supported by showing that the defendant stole a shoat.[12]

An indictment for murder which charges that the homicide was committed on the *tweflth* [sic] day of August, instead of the twelfth day of August was held to be good, if not at common law, yet at least under our statute of 1811.[13]

Where a man was indicted for stealing a "bull tongue"; and it appeared in the evidence that he had stolen a particular kind of ploughshare, usually known in the neighborhood in which he resided by that name; it was held that the allegation of the indictment was well supported by the evidence.[14]

In addition to the work of the courts in simplifying indictments during this early period, the work of the Legislature was also important. Besides the statute of 1811 (see *supra* p. 49), other statutes were passed relative to indictments for subornation of perjury, larceny of money, murder and manslaughter. These statutes will be considered more fully under the heading of Legislation (see *infra* p. 142). Without some knowledge of the extreme complexity of indictments in the early period and some knowledge of the common-law background, and the principle of *stare decisis,* one is likely to judge the courts too harshly in these days.

In the period studied forty-one cases were reversed because of defective indictments and forty cases were reversed because the lower court had quashed the indictment or arrested judgment in the belief that the indictment was defective or insufficient. It is gratifying to note that the number of defective indictments reaching the Supreme Court is only a little more than

[12] *State* v. *Godet,* 7 Ired. 210 (1847).
[13] *State* v. *Shepherd,* 8 Ired. 195 (1847).
[14] *State* v. *Clark, ibid.,* 226 (1848).

one a year. With so many possibilities for error the number is remarkably small. The number of erroneous quashals and arrests of judgment is small too in the lower courts. It is possible that a good many of these have grown out of the old theory that it is better for ninety-nine guilty men to escape punishment than for one innocent man to be punished. The state having the statutory right of appeal from a quashal or an arrest of judgment the lower courts out of abundance of caution have sometimes erred on the side of safety.

We shall now consider some of the cases where the Court has held the bill of indictment defective or insufficient. In *State* v. *Skidmore,* 109 N. C. 795 (1891), the court held that an indictment for obtaining goods by false pretense, which does not charge the offense to have been feloniously done, is defective, as the Act of 1891, chapter 205, makes all offenses punishable with death or imprisonment in the penitentiary felonies; but that the bill should not be quashed, but the defendant should be held until a new bill is obtained. The Court has consistently followed the rule of the *Skidmore* case and required the bill to charge "felonious" when the indictment is for a felony and it has set the indictment aside when the word "felonious" was omitted.[15]

There has been one important exception to this rule, however, with regard to indictments for perjury. In the cases of *State* v. *Bunting,* 118 N. C. 1200 and *State* v. *Shaw,* 117 N. C. 764, both in 1896, and both indict-

[15] *State v. Bryan,* 112 N. C. 848 (1893) ; *State v. Caldwell,* 112 N. C. 854 (1893) ; *State v. Wilson,* 116 N. C. 979 (1895) ; *State v. Snow,* 117 N. C. 774 (1895) ; *State v. Shaw,* 117 N. C. 746 (1895) ; *State v. Bunting,* 118 N. C. 1200 (1896) ; *State v. Taylor,* 131 N. C. 711 (1902) ; *State v. Brinkley,* 191 N. C. 702 (1926).

ments being for perjury, it was expressly held that the term "feloniously" was required to make a good bill of indictment for the offense. Both of these indictments were instituted after the passage of the statute of 1889 prescribing a form for bills of indictment in perjury cases (*infra* p. 146). The word "feloniously" was omitted from this form and yet seven years later we find the Supreme Court holding indictments defective which omitted the word from the bill. In the case of *State* v. *Harris,* 145 N. C. 456 (1907), the Court held that the word "feloniously" was not essential to an indictment under the *Laws of 1889,* Chapter 83. In overruling these two earlier decisions it was suggested that the lower court was evidently not advertant to the statute of 1889 for the reason probably that it did not appear in the general *Code of 1883,* and was, therefore, not called to its attention, the statute having been enacted at a subsequent session. But the law was held to be controlling and the two cases mentioned were overruled. The *Law of 1889* is still the law of the state and we are not aware that there has been any departure from it since 1896.

Another change, not very significant but making the finding of indictments a little less technical, is shown in the two following cases. In *State* v. *McBroom,* 127 N. C. 528 (1900), defendant was charged with and convicted of perjury. The Supreme Court arrested judgment because of a defective indictment. The bill was endorsed "this bill found" instead of "a true bill" and the Court held that this was a fatal defect. Justices Clark and Montgomery dissented. Then six years later in the case of *State* v. *Sutton,* 142 N. C. 569 (1906), defendant was charged with the illegal sale of spirituous liquors. From a judgment of guilty there was an appeal because a motion was refused to quash the indictment, on the ground that it did not appear that any of the witnesses before the grand jury were sworn. There was no evidence that the witnesses were not sworn, and the only defect alleged was that the blank space after "thus" in the certificate, "witnesses whose names are marked thus . . . were sworn and examined," was not filled in with a cross mark or check. Here it was held that no endorsement on a bill of indictment by a grand jury is necessary. The record that it was presented by the grand jury is sufficient in the absence of evidence to impeach it. Thus the *McBroom* case was definitely overruled.

In the following cases appeal was taken to the Supreme Court mainly on the ground of defective indictments. There are many other cases that might be included in this group but we think the following are representative and sufficient to show the attitude of the Court with regard to indictments:

In *State* v. *Harris,* 106 N. C. 682 (1890), the charge being embezzlement, the omission of the words, "with force and arms" in the bill of indictment was said to have been immaterial since the year 1546 (Statute 37 Henry VIII). . . . In this same case it was held that the defendant could not be prejudiced by an indictment concluding "against the statute."

In *State* v. *Brady,* 107 N. C. 822 (1890), it was held that in an indictment for conspiracy to cheat and defraud, the manner need not be charged.

In *State* v. *Arnold,* 107 N. C. 861 (1890), murder being charged and the word "wilfully" being omitted from the indictment, the Court held that the word was not essential to the validity of the indictment for murder, neither at common law nor under the statute 1887.

In *State* v. *Martin,* 107 N. C. 904 (1890), defendant was indicted for injury to personal property. The indictment charged that the act was "wantonly and wilfully" done. The Court sustained the indictment even though it did not aver the act to have been unlawfully perpetrated.

In *State* v. *Burke,* 108 N. C. 750 (1891), the charge was false pretense. The Court held that an indictment ought not to be quashed for want of precision or redundancy when it can be seen from the entire instrument that the charge plainly appears.

In *State* v. *Peters,* 107 N. C. 876 (1890), defendant was charged with perjury. The bill was a substantial copy of the form prescribed by the statute of 1889, Chapter 83, and it was held not to be vitiated by the addition of the formal conclusion "against the form of the statute in such cases made and provided, and against the peace and dignity of the state," for, while such conclusion is not necessary, its use is a mere surplusage.

In *State* v. *Frizell,* 111 N. C. 722 (1892), in a prosecution for an affray the indictment was drawn against the defendant and one J., and the names of these two were marked as witnesses who were sworn and examined, but a true bill was returned only as to the defendant, who moved to quash, and in arrest of judgment, on the ground that "the back of the bill showed that the defendant was a witness against himself before the grand jury." The Court held that these motions were properly refused, as, there being two defendants in the bill, the presumption was that they were examined as witnesses only against each other, and not each one against himself.

In *State* v. *Robbins,* 123 N. C. 730 (1898), an indictment was held not to be defective on the ground that it consisted of two papers, pinned together and returned as one bill, when it contained two charges designated respectively, as "First Count" and "Second Count."

In *State* v. *Tweedy,* 115 N. C. 704 (1894), defendant was

indicted for killing a hog running at large in a town in violation of the town ordinance prohibiting the running at large of hogs therein. The bill charged that the killing was done "unlawfully and on purpose." The Court held that it could not be sustained under section 1082 of the Code, where there is neither an allegation nor finding that the injury was "wilfully and unlawfully done."

In *State* v. *Harwell*, 129 N. C. 550 (1901), defendant was charged with slandering an innocent and virtuous woman under section 1113 of the Code which provides, "that if any person shall attempt, in a wanton and malicious manner, to destroy the reputation of an innocent woman, etc." and the bill of indictment charges that the defendant "unlawfully, wilfully, feloniously did attempt to destroy the reputation. . . . The bill was quashed and the state appealed. The Court held that the indictment was fatally defective because an indictment for slander of an innocent woman must charge that the defendant did attempt in a "wanton and malicious" manner to destroy the reputation of an innocent woman.

In *State* v. *Battle,* 130 N. C. 655 (1902), an indictment was held defective because it was too general. It was held that in indictments for assaults, batteries and affrays, where serious damage has been done, it is necessary to describe the serious damage done, its character and extent.

In *State* v. *Ratliff,* 170 N. C. 707 (1915), it was held that where an indictment for seduction under promise of marriage conforms with the statute except in the charge that the prosecutrix was an "innocent and virtuous" woman, omitting the word "and," the omission does not make the indictment fatally defective, for the expressions used supply the omission, and a motion to quash will be refused; and as a comma between the words "innocent" and "virtuous" would have the same effect, it would be the same as if the indictment had been imperfectly punctuated, which is not material.

As has already been indicated (see *supra* p. 52), technicalities, hair splitting distinctions and over-refinements have been most apparent in the matter of indictments. A study of the cases year by year shows a progressive tendency on the part of the courts and an attempt to rid indictments of non-essentials. In the future it is to be expected that there will be fewer and fewer cases reversed for defective indictments.

QUASHED INDICTMENTS

Table VI[16] shows that forty cases were reversed because the trial judge either quashed the indictment or arrested judgment in the belief that the indictment was fatally defective. While in the aggregate the number appears to be large, in reality it is not, when distributed over the entire period of thirty-eight years. It would not be worth while to take up all the cases where there has been an erroneous quashal or arrest of judgment, but we shall consider some of the most interesting ones to show the possibility of error and some of the complexities the courts have had to face.

In *State* v. *Eaves,* 106 N. C. 752 (1890), defendant was charged with violating a statute which prohibited the sale of spirituous liquors within three miles of "Rutherfordton Baptist Church in the county of Rutherford." The indictment charged the sale of one quart of spirituous liquors within three miles of the *old site* of Rutherford Baptist Church, etc. The jury returned a verdict of guilty but the court arrested judgment on the ground that the indictment was defective in not setting forth the fact that the church had been removed since the passage of the statute. The judge reasoned that since the law was passed to protect the church and since the church had been removed the old site

[16]See *supra,* p. 33.

needed no protection and that the law was inoperative. But on appeal, the Supreme Court held the indictment valid, set the judgment aside and remanded the case.

In *State* v. *Haddock,* 109 N. C. 873 (1891), the trial judge quashed an indictment as defective for slandering an innocent and virtuous woman which charged that the defendant "did, by words spoken, declare in substance that the said L. B. was an incontinent woman." The quashal was held to be erroneous as this was a sufficient description of the offense charged, notwithstanding the alleged slanderous words were not set out.

In *State* v. *Sharp,* 110 N. C. 604 (1892), on an indictment for larceny of corn the trial judge quashed the bill and the state appealed. It was held to be error to quash merely because the son of the prosecutor, was a member of the grand jury, and actively participated in finding the bill.

In *State* v. *Mangum,* 116 N. C. 998 (1895), false pretense being charged, the bill was quashed as being fatally defective and the state appealed. It was held that a bill of indictment which charged that the defendant in swapping stated that his horse was sound, knowing that he was not sound, and that the prosecutor was induced thereby to trade, is sufficient since it charges that the defendant misrepresented a subsisting fact calculated to cheat and which the state says did cheat, etc.

In *State* v. *Peak,* 130 N. C. 711 (1902), the trial judge quashed a bill of indictment charging an assault with intent to commit rape because the word "forcibly" was omitted. On appeal it was held that such an indictment in order to be valid need not contain the word forcibly. In *State* v. *Powell,* 106 N. C. 635, (1890), the omission of the words "against her will" were held to invalidate the indictment which charged an assault with intent to commit rape, etc.

Thus it would seem that the *Powell* case was overruled by the decision in the *Peak* case. But the next year in *State* v. *Marsh,* 132 N. C. 1000 (1903), where the indictment was for rape, we find the Court holding that the bill must charge that the act was done forcibly and against the will of the prosecutrix, or words equivalent thereto. The law seems a little confused on this matter at the present time. Since there are statutory provisions governing indictments in several of the other leading felonies it seems the Legislature might very well clear this matter up by law.

In *State* v. *Lewis,* 142 N. C. 626 (1906), lynching being charged, it was held to be an error to quash a bill of indictment under *Revisal,* section 3698, which charged the defendant with conspiring "with others" to commit the crime of lynching because it did not name the others or charge that they were unknown.

VARIANCE BETWEEN THE ALLEGATION AND THE PROOF

Table VI[17] shows that eight cases were reversed by the Supreme Court on the ground that there was a fatal variance between the allegation and the proof. We shall first consider some of the cases where the variance was held to be fatal:

In *State* v. *Gibson,* 169 N. C. 318 (1915), the indictment charged obtaining money by false pretense and the state's evidence tended to show that the defendant had obtained the signature of the prosecutor as an indorser or security to a negotiable instrument under the assertion that others, whose responsibility was known to him, had promised to sign, as cosecurities and should sign before negotiation, which was in all respects false, etc. The variance was held to be fatal.

In *State* v. *McWhirter,* 141 N. C. 809 (1906), the defendant was charged with obtaining from the prosecutor by certain false representations a note and mortgage, but all the evidence tended to show that the prosecutor did not

[17] See *supra,* p. 33.

surrender said note and mortgage and so it was held that there was a fatal variance between the allegation and the proof.

In *State* v. *Harbert,* 185 N. C. 760 (1923), it was held that a defendant in a criminal prosecution has a constitutional right to be informed of the accusation against him, and he must be convicted if at all, of the offense charged in the bill of indictment; and when he has been indicted for the larceny of an automoblie owned and in the possession of A., and the proof is that B was such owner there is a fatal variance between the allegation and proof.

State v. *Hill,* 79 N. C. 656 (1878), was cited by the Court in the Harbert case with apparent approval. In the Hill case the defendant was charged with injuring a cow and the proof was that the animal injured was an ox. This was held to be a fatal variance.

In *State* v. *Corpening,* 191 N. C. 751 (1926), the Court held that an indictment charging the defendant with obtaining money on a day named by the issuance of a worthless check in violation of our statute, and evidence that it was given for hire of an automobile, ten days later, are at fatal variance and will not support a conviction.

In *State* v. *Davis,* 150 N. C. 851 (1908), the defendant was charged with obtaining a clay-bank mare by means of false pretense as to the qualities of a "sorrel-horse," and the proof was that he obtained the clay-bank mare in exchange for a bay "saddle horse." This was held to be a material variance.

The Court no doubt had sufficient reason to reverse the cases just given. It is surprising, though, that in 1923 the Court should have cited with apparent approval such an absurd decision as the Hill case, thus keeping it alive.

On the other hand, there was held to be no fatal variance in the following cases:

In *State* v. *Ogleston,* 177 N. C. 541 (1919), defendant was charged with manufacturing spirituous liquors, and was convicted for aiding and abetting therein. The Court upheld the conviction under the Laws of 1917, chapter 157.

In *State* v. *Simmons,* 179 N. C. 700 (1920), the Court held that an indictment charging arson by the defendant as principal included the charge of arson as accessory before the fact, so that a judgment accepting a plea of guilty as accessory under such an indictment and sentencing the defendant is legal.

In *State* v. *Grier,* 184 N. C. 723 (1922), it was held that a conviction might be had under *C. S. s.* 3409, making it a misdemeanor to manufacture or aid and abet in the manufacture of intoxicants, for aiding and abetting though the bill charged only the manufacture, notwithstanding the offense charged is but a statutory misdemeanor.

In *State* v. *Overcash,* 182 N. C. 889 (1921), where the defendants were charged with larceny, it was held that unless time was of the essence of the offense charged, a variance between the allegation and proof as to the time is immaterial, and the prosecution, unless otherwise required by the court, is not restricted to the time charged, but may offer evidence as to the commission of the offense at the time before the indictment and within the period of the statute of limitations.

In *State* v. *Hester,* 122 N. C. 1047 (1898), the indictment charged perjury in an action wherein one "H. was plaintiff and Thos. R. Robertson was defendant." The proof showed that "Thomas Robertson" was defendant in said action and there was held to be no variance.

In *State* v. *Drakeford,* 162 N. C. 667 (1913), where defendant was indicted for rape, the bill of indictment showed the name of the prosecutrix to be Lila H. when the proof showed that it was Liza H. This was held at most to be an immaterial variance.

In *State* v. *Railroad,* 149 N. C. 508 (1908), the defendant company was charged with running trains on Sunday. The proof tended to show that the offense occurred in July, and the charge assigned the date as January following. This was held to be no fatal variance.

CHAPTER VI

INSTRUCTIONS TO THE JURY

TABLE VI[1] shows 231 reversals because of errors in instructing the jury. Properly instructing a jury is indeed a difficult and painstaking task. The average citizen who visits a courtroom and hears the judge instructing the jury has little idea of the responsibility resting upon the trial judge, or the difficulty of his task. His duty is rendered still more difficult of fulfillment by certain statutory provisions and by judicial precedent. In 1796 a statute was passed and is still in effect, which forbade the judge at any time during the trial to express an opinion on the weight of the evidence or to make any remark from which an inference could be drawn as to his opinion of the facts.[2] This statute is simple in form but difficult of application. No matter how strongly the judge may feel that the defendant is guilty or innocent he must, for the time being at least, lay aside all personal prejudice and speak impartially. In addition to the statutory limitations the Supreme Court has added restrictions from time to time. A charge that appeared to be fair and in conformity with the statute on its face, has sometimes been held to be opinionated and prejudicial, and therefore to constitute a reversible error.

[1] See *supra*, p. 33.

[2] No judge in giving a charge to a petit jury, whether in a civil or criminal action, shall give an opinion whether a fact is fully or sufficiently proven, that being the office and province of the jury; but he shall state in a plain and correct manner the evidence given in the case, and declare and explain the law arising thereon. (1796, c. 452, sec. 51; *Consolidated Statutes*, sec. 564.)

ATTITUDE OF THE SUPREME COURT

We shall now consider a number of cases which will probably throw some light on the attitude of the Supreme Court with regard to what is considered as being a fair and correct charge and what is regarded as being reversibly erroneous. A few cases will also be considered in an attempt to show something of the trends and tendencies of the Court with regard to instructing the jury.

In *State* v. *Davis,* 136 N. C. 568 (1904), defendant was indicted for an assault with a deadly weapon. On appeal a new trial was ordered because the trial judge made the statement during the trial that the witness had fully explained for an hour to the jury and to the satisfaction of the court certain facts. This was held to be an expression of opinion prohibited by the statute.

In *State* v. *Williams,* 172 N. C. 894 (1916), defendant was being tried for an assault upon one of his pupils. In the course of his charge to the jury the judge said, "I think if we would go back to the old whipping post we would have less crime in the land than we have got now. But school teachers have got no right to take a boy and sling him up against the house and bruise or make a bruise on him. . . ." The Court ordered a new trial on the ground that this was a strong expression of opinion in violation of the statute.

In *State* v. *Horne,* 171 N. C. 787 (1916), defendant was convicted of murder in the first degree. A new trial was ordered because the trial judge commented upon the "admirably lucid" testimony of an expert witness. This expression was held to be stronger than the statute permitted and so constituted a reversible error.

In the following cases expressions by the court were held not to be an expression of opinion prohibited by the statute:

In *State* v. *Jacobs,* 106 N. C. 695 (1890), defendant was charged with murder. On appeal it was held that a remark by the trial judge, made before the trial began, that the jailor had informed him that the prisoner "would escape if he had the opportunity" is not an expression of opinion upon the facts prohibited by the Act of 1796.

In *State* v. *Howard,* 129 N. C. 584 (1901), defendant was indicted for conspiracy to cheat and defraud by false pretenses, etc. On appeal a remark of the trial judge complimentary to the character of one of the witnesses in the case, made before the jury was empanelled, was held not to be prohibited by common law or by the Code, sec. 413.

In *State* v. *Journigan,* 120 N. C. 568 (1897), it was held that a charge that perjury is very much a matter of intent, and as to that the jury must be satisfied beyond reasonable doubt upon "all the facts and circumstances of the case deposed to by witnesses" contains no expression of opinion by the judge.

In *State* v. *Robertson,* 121 N. C. 551 (1897), defendant was charged with seduction. The response of the prosecutrix to a question provoked boisterous laughter from the crowd of bystanders. The trial judge in attempting to quell the disturbance remarked, "If I could discover the infernal fiends who laugh in such a manner I would send them to jail for contempt." Such remarks were held not to be an expression of opinion on the facts involved in the prosecution.

In *State* v. *Rowe,* 155 N. C. 436 (1911), defendant was charged with murder and convicted of manslaughter. On appeal to the Supreme Court, it was held not to be a reversible error for the trial judge to tell the sheriff in the presence of the jury, after four counsel had addressed them, the last being one of the defendant's, "You may give the jury water, and, gentlemen of the jury, if you wish to retire to your room you can do so for a few minutes. We have no band to play between the speeches."

From the above cited cases and others which might be mentioned it seems that the Court has been careful to see that the provisions of the statute prohibiting an expression of opinion by the court on the weight or value of the evidence has been fully complied with. Though there have been many reversals for the violation of this statute, the cases show that they have been inadvertent rather than intentional for the most part.

This statute prohibiting the judge from expressing an opinion upon the weight of the evidence is a radical departure from the common-law practice. Whether the statute has improved criminal procedure or not is open to very grave doubt with most of the evidence indicating that it has not. Sir Matthew Hale, writing 1671, or earlier, of the characteristics of trial by jury said:

Tenthly, another excellency of this trial is this: that the judge is always present at the time of the evidence given in it. Herein he is able, in matters of law emerging upon the evidence, to direct them; and also, in matters of fact to give them great light and assistance by his weighing the evidence before them, and observing where the question and knot of business lies, and by shewing them his opinion even in matter of fact; which is a great advantage and light to lay-men. And thus, as the jury assists the judge in determining the matter of fact, so the judge assists the jury in determining points of law, and also very much in investigating and enlightening the matter of fact, whereof the jury are judges.[3]

In the Federal Courts the privilege of expressing an opinion on the weight of the evidence is unimpaired, but the great majority of Federal trial judges follow

[3] Matthew Hale, *History of the Common Law of England,* p. 291 (4th ed., Dublin, 1792).

the state practice and refrain from expressing an opinion. But the Supreme Court of the United States has said :

Trial by jury in the primary and usual sense of the term at the common law and in American constitutions . . . is a trial by a jury of twelve men, in the presence and under the superintendence of a judge empowered to instruct them on the law and to advise them on the facts.[4]

It seems that if the real purpose of a trial is to ascertain the truth instead of encouraging a mere contest of skill between opposing counsel the judge should be permitted to express an opinion on the weight of the evidence. The judge is skilled in weighing evidence and finding facts, but unlike the counsel, he is unprejudiced, impartial and disinterested. Furthermore, the jurors are inexperienced and do not have the training which enables them to distinguish the issues from the mass of conflicting evidence and the perversions of fact by counsel. If the judge is forbidden to comment upon the evidence, the only person connected with the trial who is both disinterested and intellectually qualified to ascertain the facts and to set forth the issues has his hands tied and must sit silently by while two lawyers match their wits to confuse the issues and facts in the minds of the jurors. The jurors look in vain to the judge for assistance but get only a legal essay which to them is practically meaningless. Undoubtedly justice would be greatly promoted and in no way would the province of the jury be invaded if the judge were invested with the power of expressing an opinion on the weight of the evidence.

The following cases show something of the change in

[4] *Capital Traction Co.* v. *Hof,* 174 U. S. 1 (1898).

the attitude of the Supreme Court with regard to the giving of instructions. As intimated by the Court in the *Beard* case (see *infra* p. 73) the idea has been to break away from formalism and make instructing the jury a more simple matter.

In the older case of *State* v. *Boyle,* 104 N. C. 800 (1889), rape being charged, the Court held that the statute of 1796 was mandatory and that the only cases in which it might be dispensed with were those where the evidence was un-contradictory and the law plain. It was further held that this duty was not performed by simply repeating the testimony in the order in which it was delivered, or in a general statement of the principles of law applicable to the case; but it requires the judge to state clearly and distinctly the particular issues arising in the controversy; to eliminate the controverted facts; to arraign the testimony in its bearing on the different aspects, and to instruct the jury as to the law applicable thereto in such manner as will enable them to see and comprehend the matters which are essential to an intelligent and impartial verdict.

A year later in the case of *State v. Pritchett,* 106 N. C. 667 (1890), the Court modified its opinion somewhat and broke rather abruptly with the rule in the Boyle case. Here the defendant was convicted of murder. In affirming the decision of lower court it was said that failure to "state in a plain and correct manner the evidence given in the case and declare and explain the law arising thereon," is not error when the court is not requested to do so, especially when the evidence is neither complicated or peculiar in its bearings, and when the court expressly directs attention to evidence in defendant's behalf.

This case was followed several years later (1897), by *State* v. *Groves,* 121 N. C. 536. In this case defendant was convicted of murder in the second degree. In ordering a new trial the Court referred to the Statute of 1796, and declared that a charge to a jury, in the trial of an indictment for murder, where the evidence of guilt is conflicting, is insufficient which clearly defines the different degrees of murder and contains no array of the facts or instruction as to the law applicable to such facts as the jury may find to be true from the evidence. Although the defendant gives his consent that the judge need not read over his notes of the testimony, there was not a waiver of his right to have the law applied to the facts in his case as the law requires.

Then in 1899, in the case of *State* v. *Beard,* 124 N. C. 811, the matter was cleared up and the Boyle case was criticised and overruled. Furches, J. speaking for the Court said, "*State* v. *Boyle,* has been so often criticised, explained, and overruled on the point for which it is cited that it can no longer be considered as authority. The Court in that case undertook to say how well a judge should succeed in aiding the jury to understand the evidence, and seems to have succeeded better in producing confusion than in establishing the rule of practice intended to be established. We do not wish to fall into this error again. It is true that the object of the charge is to state the law of the case to the jury, and to aid them in applying the facts to the law; but the manner in which this is to be done must be left, to a very great extent to the good sense and sound judgment of the judge who tries the case.

The rule of the *Baker* case is the rule of law in North Carolina. A casual examination of the cases leaves some doubt in the mind of the reader as to whether the rule of *Boyle* prevails or whether the Court is still following the rule of the *Baker* case. But a careful reading of the cases shows that an instruction is not erroneous merely because the court failed to charge on some particular phase of the evidence, or because the court completely omitted certain phases of the evidence from the charge, unless there was a written request from counsel to have the matter presented. On the other hand the rule seems clear that failure to charge on the various aspects of the law involved in the case is a reversible error whether there is a request to so instruct or not.

In *State* v. *Teachy,* 138 N. C. 587 (1905), defendant was convicted of murder in the first degree. On appeal to the Supreme Court it was held that failure of the court to charge the jury on the question of manslaughter was not prejudicial to him as there was no evidence to show manslaughter.

In *State* v. *Merrick,* 171 N. C. 788 (1916), defendant was convicted of murder in the first degree. In ordering a new trial the Court held that the judge must charge on the different aspects presented by the evidence and should give the law applicable to every state of facts which may be reasonably assumed. The trial judge had entirely omitted from his charge the question of manslaughter and this was a reversible error.[5]

INTRICACIES AND TECHNICALITIES

Some of the intricacies and technicalities of instructing the jury are illustrated in the following cases:

In *State* v. *Barrett,* 123 N. C. 753 (1898), the charge being larceny, the Court in ordering a new trial held that a charge was fatally defective which did not submit the question of felonious intent to the jury, as that is one of the essential ingredients of larceny. . . . It was held in the same case that the proper expression to be used in a charge to the jury should be: "If you find from the evidence such to be the fact, or facts," instead of: "If you believe such a fact or facts," which is often but improperly used.

[5] Other cases involving this point are: *State* v. *Kale,* 124 N. C. 816 (1899); *State* v. *Baum,* 128 N. C. 601 (1901); *State* v. *Godwin,* 145 N. C. 461 (1907); *State* v. *Kennedy,* 169-288 (1915); *State* v. *Kendall,* 143 N. C. 659 (1907); *State* v. *Foster,* 130 N. C. 666 (1902).

In *State* v. *Godwin,* 145 N. C. 461 (1907), a misdemeanor being charged, it was held to be error in the trial judge to charge the jury peremptorily to find the defendant guilty upon a certain phase of the testimony, without directing them to pass upon the evidence or credibility of the witness. The instruction should have been based upon their belief of the evidence, or, which is better in form, upon their finding of facts in accordance with the evidence.

In *State* v. *Rollins,* 113 N. C. 722 (1893), defendant was convinced of felonious slaying and upon appeal the Court affirmed the instruction that if the jury believed a certain state of facts as deposed to by certain witnesses the law applicable is so and so, for thus the attention of the jury was directed not to the credibility of the witnesses, but to a certain state of facts or hypothesis.

In *State* v. *Woodard,* 119 N. C. 779 (1896), defendant was convicted of abandonment and appealed to the Supreme Court on the ground of improper instruction to the jury. The decision of the lower court was affirmed and the Court said, "when justified by the evidence the judge may charge the jury that if they believe the testimony of the defendant, who testified in his own behalf, that they should find him guilty."

In *State* v. *Moore,* 192 N. C. 209 (1926), defendant was convicted of violating the prohibition law. One witness testified that he bought a pint of whisky from the defendant and paid him two dollars for it. This evidence was uncontradicted. The trial judge instructed the jury that if they believed the evidence of this witness beyond a reasonable doubt that they should find the defendant guilty. This instruction was approved by the Supreme Court, and the case was affirmed.

It was contended that this instruction was erroneous; but there was no other evidence of the transaction and the evidence if believed was susceptible of only one construction, that is, that the defendant made the sale, and under such circumstances similar instructions have been repeatedly sustained. It was further held that the rule did not apply where the evidence, if true, was susceptible of more than one deduction. In distinguishing this case and the case of *State* v. *Hardy,* 189 N. C. 799 (1925), in which upon assignments of error a new trial was awarded the Court said, "There the instruction, if you believe the evidence as testified you will return a verdict of guilty was disapproved; but the evidence to which the instruction referred was regarded as open to more than one construction. . . ." In any event *Hardy's* case cannot be reasonably interpreted as conflicting with the long line of decisions which have upheld the principle now under discussion.

Special Circumstances Requiring Instruction

Prior to 1881 the law did not regard the testimony of a man charged with a crime as fit to be submitted to the jury. Nevertheless, a number of cases arose in which there was manifest injustice; so the Legislature of that year very properly passed a law allowing any person charged with a crime, even though the conviction would forfeit his life, to go upon the witness stand and testify in his own behalf.[6] When the defendant

[6] In the trial of all indictments, complaints or other proceedings against persons charged with the commission of crimes, offenses and misdemeanors, the person so charged shall at his own request, but not otherwise, be a competent witness, and his failure to make such request shall not create any presumption against him. But every such person examined as a witness shall be subject to cross examination as other witnesses. Except as above provided, nothing in this section shall render any person, who in any criminal proceeding is charged with the commission of any criminal offense, competent or compellable to give evidence against himself nor render any person compellable to answer any question tending to criminate himself. 1868-69, c. 209, sec. 4; 1881, c. 110; *Consolidated Statutes,* sec. 1799.

testifies in his own behalf, usually some caution or instruction to the jury is necessary as to the weight to be given to the testimony in making up their decision and verdict.

In the early case of *State* v. *Byers,* 100 N. C. 512 (1888), the Court held that where a prisoner and his relatives, or an associate in the crime, testify on behalf of the prisoner, the law directs the jury to scrutinize their testimony carefully, because of their interest in the result; and the judge may so caution the jury, although a failure so to do is not assignable as error.

In *State* v. *Bynum,* 175 N. C. 777 (1918), defendant was convicted of murder in the first degree. On appeal the Supreme Court found no error, observing that while the failure of the prisoner to take the witness-stand voluntarily will not create a presumption against him, the fact that he did not testify, under the circumstances of the case, was a circumstance though not evidence, which with the evidence introduced may have had some weight with the jury.

In *State* v. *Burton,* 172 N. C. 939 (1916), a homicide case, the Supreme Court affirmed a charge as follows: "When you come to consider the evidence of the defendant himself, remember his relation to the case as defendant, the interest which he has in the result of your verdict, and to scrutinize his testimony with care, to the end that you may determine to what extent if any, his testimony has been biased by his interest."

In *State* v. *Tucker,* 190 N. C. 708 (1925), defendant was tried and convicted of violating the prohibition law. A new trial was granted on appeal because the prosecuting attorney was permitted to argue to the jury that the prisoner who had not taken the stand looked like a professional bootlegger. . . . It was also held in this case that the legal presumption in favor of the defendant in a criminal action goes with him throughout the trial, and that failure to take the witness stand in his own behalf should not prejudice him.

There are other cases on this point, but it is unnecessary to discuss them. The Court has been consistent in upholding the statute with hardly an exception. It is interesting to note the few cases from the lower courts that have been reversed for violation of this statute. It should be noted that this statute has been held to apply to the trial judge only and not to the prosecuting attorney. In *State* v. *Harrison,* 145 N. C. 408 (1907) the Court said, "We undertake to correct the errors committed by the judge and not those committed by the attorneys."

The weight to be given to testimony of near relatives is not regulated by statute in this state. In 1847 the matter was settled by the Supreme Court and is now a rule of law with as much force as if there were a statutory provision.

In the case of *State* v. *Nash,* 30 N. C. 35 (1847), where defendant was on trial for murder, the mother of the prisoner, being introduced by him to prove an alibi, the court charged the jury that the law regarded with suspicion the testimony of near relatives when testifying for each other; that it was the province of the jury to consider and decide on the weight due her testimony, and as a general rule, in deciding on the credit of the witness on both sides, they ought to look to the deportment of the witnesses, their capacity and opportunity to testify in relation to the transaction, and the relation in which the witness stood to the party.

The competency of the husband or wife as witness for and against each other is regulated by the statute of 1881.[7]

[7] The husband or wife of the defendant, in all criminal actions or proceedings shall be a competent witness for the defendant, but the failure of such witness to be examined shall

In *State* v. *Cox,* 150 N. C. 846 (1909), defendant was convicted of incest. The State tendered the wife of defendant as witness and the solicitor commented upon the refusal of defendant to use her in corroboration of his own evidence. Upon objection by defendant, it became the duty of the trial judge to caution the jury that this refusal of the accused should not be considered by them, and failure to so caution was a reversible error; and his telling them that the state could not use the wife as a witness, but the accused could, was an unintentional accentuation of the error.[8]

Instruction to the jury with regard to recently stolen goods has often been before the Court. In the case of *State* v. *Graves,* 72 N. C. 482 (1875), Chief Justice Pearson stated the rule as follows:

When goods are stolen, one found in possession so soon thereafter that he could not have reasonably got the possession unless he had stolen them himself, the law presumes he was a thief. This is simply a declaration of common sense, and when the fact is so plain that there can be no mistake about it, our courts following the practice of the courts in England, where the judge is allowed to express his opinion as to the weight of the evidence, have adopted it as a rule of law, which the judge is at liberty to act on, notwithstanding the statute which forbids a judge from intimating an opinion as to the weight of the evidence. But the rule, like that of *falsum in uno, falsum in omnibus,* and

not be used to the prejudice of the defense. Every such person examined as a witness shall be subject to be cross examined as are other witnesses. No husband or wife shall be compellable to disclose any confidential communication made by one to the other during their marriage . . . 1881, c. 110. *Consolidated Statutes,* sec. 1802.

[8] Other cases involving this statute are: *State* v. *Fulton,* 149 N. C. 485 (1908); *State* v. *Brittain,* 117 N. C. 783 (1895); *State* v. *Randall,* 170 N. C. 757 (1915); *State* v. *Record,* 151 N. C. 695 (1909); *State* v. *Spivey,* 151, N. C. 676 (1909).

the presumption of fraud, as a matter of law from certain fiduciary relations has been reduced to very narrow proportions, and is never applicable when it is necessary to resort to other evidence to support the conclusion; in other words the fact of guilt must be *self evident* from the *bare fact* of being found in the possession of the stolen goods, in order to justify the judge in laying it down as a presumption made by law; otherwise it is a case depending on circumstantial evidence, to be passed on by the jury.

The rule laid down by Chief Justice Pearson has become the settled law of the Court in this state. There is a long line of cases which follow this rule in the main. The rule has been broadened somewhat giving the defendant better opportunity to rebut the evidence. In *State* v. *Anderson,* 162 N. C. 571 (1913), the Court also added that it must be manifest that the stolen goods have come to the possession by his own act or with his undoubted concurrence, and it must be so recent and under such circumstance as to give reasonable assurance that such possession could not have been obtained unless the holder is himself the thief. This law has already had a new application in regard to stolen automobiles and is likely to be still further developed and applied.

Erroneous Statement of the Contentions of the Parties

From time to time there have been appeals because of what purported to be an erroneous statement of the contentions of the parties in a case. Sometimes claims have been made that the statement was prejudicial, while in other instances it was claimed that the contentions of the parties were stated more favorably to one party than to the other. Up until 1923, it was uniformly

upheld that if the court recited the evidence or contentions of the parties incorrectly, any objection must be
made at the time so as to give judge opportunity to
correct it, and that otherwise the objection is waived.[9]

But in *State* v. *Love,* 187 N. C. 32 (1923), the Court
held that the rule requiring an objection to be made at
the time of the charge to an erroneous statement of the
contentions of the parties, does not apply to the trial
of first degree murder, when such statement includes
the assumption of erroneous evidence against the prisoner upon the trial, that had been excluded, tending to
show previous malice to the prisoner, vitally necessary
upon the question of his premeditation.

Chief Justice Clark dissented and condemned this
departure from the rule of the Court, and by the time of
the *Johnson* case the Court seemed to have returned to
the old rule.

In *State* v. *Johnson,* 193 N. C. 701 (1927), it was held
that when the trial judge has stated the contentions of the
opposing party, the appellant insisting upon a prejudicial
error therein must have called it to the attention of the
judge at the time to give him an opportunity for correc-
tion, or the matter will not be considered on appeal.

In *State* v. *Whaley,* 191 N. C. 387 (1926), it was held
that the contentions of parties to an action were not a necessary part of the instructions to the jury and that an error
not excepted to at the proper time would not be considered
on appeal.

WRITTEN INSTRUCTIONS

With regard to prayers for instructions to the jury,
it is provided by statute that if either party to an action,

[9] *State* v. *Cox,* 153 N. C. 638 (1910) ; *State* v. *Blackwell,* 162
N. C. 672 (1913) ; *State* v. *Fogleman,* 164 N. C. 458 (1913) ;
State v. *Cameron,* 166 N. C. 379 (1914).

requests in apt time, that the judge put his instructions to the jury in writing he must do so and read them to the jury. Such written instructions then become a part of the record. It is also provided that if either party so requests he must allow the jury to take them on their retirement and the jury must return them to the court with their verdict.[10] All requests for instruction must be in writing or the judge may disregard them. They must be filed with the clerk as a part of the record.[11]

Many appeals have grown out of these statutes. If the judge fails to instruct as requested, the aggrieved party has a right to note exceptions. Counsel have no doubt abused the statute by filing prayers for impossible and absurd instructions but in the main the trial judge has wisely ignored them. These statutes have surely contributed something to the administration of justice, for by this means the counsel have been able to bring to the attention of the judge and jury salient points which would probably have escaped the court altogether. Very naturally the judge will seriously consider them, and if

[10] The judge at the request of any party to an action on trial, made at or before the close of the evidence, before instructing the jury on the law, must put his instructions in writing and read them to the jury; he shall then sign and file them with the clerk as a part of the record of the action.

When the judge puts his instructions in writing either of his own will or at the request of a party to an action, he must at the request of either party to the action, allow the jury to take his instructions with them on their retirement, and the jury must return the instructions with their verdict to the court. 1885, c. 137. *Consolidated Statutes,* sec. 566.

[11] Counsel praying of the judge instructions to the jury, must put their requests in writing entitled of the cause and sign them; otherwise the judge may disregard them. They must be filed with the clerk as a part of the record. *Revisal,* sec. 538; *Consolidated Statutes,* sec. 565.

the prayer is for a worthy instruction it will be given under pains of having the case appealed to the Supreme Court for failure to instruct the jury. It is useless to speculate as to whether the judge is more cautious in a charge which he has to write out and which becomes part of the record than he is when he is merely giving an oral charge. Whether an injustice would result because the judge would have a tendency to give more attention to the written parts of his instruction to the neglect of the unwritten parts is purely a speculative matter. But it would be a bad policy to require the judge to give only instructions prayed for and no others.

Instruction That Is Uninstructive

More cases have been reversed because of improper instructions to the jury than for any other reason. While the laws on the subject are not perfect, it is indeed difficult to locate the special weaknesses of the system. Perhaps one of the most vital weaknesses of all is that much of the instruction is uninstructive. A charge to the jury may fulfill all the legal requirements and yet, so far as instructing the jury is concerned, it may be of little or no value. As a rule jurors are not trained in the law, and if they were, there is little evidence that the judge's charge would be any more keenly appreciated. The jury is faced with the practical problem of rendering a legal verdict upon the evidence submitted in the case. A few simple statements from the court with regard to the law would probably be of great value in reaching the verdict. But it often happens that the judge makes a few introductory or prefatory remarks and then settles down to reading from lifeless pages and former decisions. Many of these are veiled in legal terms which mean little or nothing to the jury. It would be difficult to find more unreadable or uninteresting printed matter. The charge may conform to the law in every particular and yet not be worthwhile. Stereotyped and formal charges have already been carried to an extreme and there is great need of breaking away from mere form and instructing the jury in a simple way upon the principles of law to be applied in the case. This is a matter that the judges themselves can do a great deal to remedy. It is easier for the Supreme Court to adopt a charge as a sort of model and sustain all charges as correct which conform to this standard, but so long as this plan is followed so long will there be dull charges to sleepy juries. There must be some form and regularity in legal proceedings, but the end sought is justice and it is more to be desired than form. If form is inconsistent with justice, then, by all means, the form should be changed or abolished for the sake of justice.

As appears from the statute providing for court stenographers (see *infra* p. 155), the matter of employing a court stenographer to keep full records of the proceedings is left to the discretion of the trial judge, unless there happens to be a county stenographer. This statute should be made mandatory and a complete record of the proceedings kept. Since the stenographer would have to take down the charge in full, there would be less likelihood of errors and inaccuracies in the records going up to the Supreme Court. It would be well also to require that the main points in each charge be written down and given to the jury to take with them on their retirement. When the jury retires, often the only thing they carry with them is the complicated maze of the judge's instruction abounding in legal phrases and technicalities. A written summary of the main points involved would probably speed up the work of the jury and prevent the introduction of many extraneous questions which result only in a loss of time.

CHAPTER VII

ERRORS IN ADMITTING OR EXCLUDING EVIDENCE

TABLE VI[1] indicates that seventy-six cases were reversed either because proper evidence had been excluded or because improper evidence had been admitted in the trial of the case in the lower court. A casual glance at the part of the Constitution and the laws of the state governing evidence might lead one to expect that the rules of evidence are rather simple, but in reality nothing could be further from the truth. In a limited study of this kind it is impossible to give a satisfactory treatment of evidence since volumes might be written upon it. Many interesting cases must be omitted because they are more or less isolated, and there are not enough cases to show any decided trends or tendencies of the Court. Where there are only a few cases illustrating some common rule of evidence, it seems that a digest or restatement of the law would serve no useful purpose; so the discussions will be confined to a few general headings in an attempt to show what the Court regards as inadmissible evidence. Where important changes have occurred in the statutes or decisions of the Court they will be noted.

One of the most difficult problems of the trial judge is to decide quickly and impartially important rules of evidence under high pressure from the counsel. Lockhart, on *Evidence,* says:

In this state all preliminary questions as to the competency of the witness and the admissibility of evidence are decided by the judge. He says whether or not a certain wit-

[1] See *supra,* p. 33.

ness can testify, and whether or not certain evidence may be admitted. Witnesses testify to him as to the competency of a witness and as to the admissibility of evidence. While the witnesses are testifying, he may send the jury out of the room, if to do so would, in his discretion be desirable. In case of confessions, the judge decides as to whether or not they are voluntary before they are admitted in evidence, and he may call as many witnesses as he desires in order to determine the matter, and the jury have no concern with the confession till the judge decides it is voluntary. And these preliminary findings of fact by the judge are conclusive on appeal to the Supreme Court. But as to whether the facts so found are sufficient to warrant the admission of the confession in evidence, is a question of law which may be reviewed on appeal. The judge says whether or not certain acts are a part of the *res gestae* so as to be admissible . . . whether the declarations of the deceased were made under such circumstances as to be admissible as dying declarations, and whether or not witness is an expert. In these preliminary matters, the findings of the judge are conclusive, if there is any evidence to warrant such findings.[2]

Most of the reversals have grown out of the rules with regard to: testimony against self, confessions, character, husband or wife of defendant, co-defendants, collateral offenses and newly discovered evidence.

Against Self

The Constitution, Article I, Section 11, provides that no person shall be compelled to give evidence against himself. In connection with this section it may be well to consider the following statute which was passed 1868-69 and is now Section 1799 of the *Consolidated Statutes:*

[2] W. S. Lockhart, *Handbook of Evidence for N. C.,* sec. 11, p. 8 (Cincinnati, 1915).

In the trial of all criminal indictments, complaints, or other proceedings against persons charged with the commission of crimes, offenses or misdemeanors, the person so charged is, at his own request but not otherwise, a competent witness, and his failure to make such request shall not create any presumption against him. But every such person examined as a witness shall be subject to cross examination as other witnesses except as above provided, nothing in this section shall render any person, who in a criminal proceeding is charged with the commission of a criminal offense, competent or compellable to give evidence against himself, nor render any person compellable to answer any question tending to criminate himself.

Some of the leading cases interpreting and construing the above section and statute are given below:

In *Smith* v. *Smith,* 116 N. C. 285 (1895), it was held that the true intent and meaning of Article I, Section 11 of the state Constitution is that a witness shall not be compelled to answer any question, the answer to which would disclose a fact which forms an essential link in the chain of testimony which would be sufficient to convict him of a crime. Chief Justice Faircloth, delivering the opinion said, "We think the provisions of our Constitution ought to be liberally construed to preserve personal rights and to protect the citizen against self-incriminating evidence."

Speaking of the above statute in *State* v. *Bynum,* 175 N. C. 777 (1918), the Court said:

Formerly the defendant in a criminal proceeding was not allowed to go upon the stand in his own defense. But under our act of 1881, the person charged shall at his own request, but not otherwise, be a competent witness, and his failure to make such request shall not create any presumption against him. This latter clause is omitted from the statute in England and in most of our states, in which failure of the defendant to testify in a criminal action raises presumption against him as in a civil action.

In *State* v. *Morgan,* 133 N. C. 743 (1903), defendant was charged with keeping a gaming house and playing at cards a game of chance for money. The first witness for the state was asked if he ever saw any cards played in the room of the defendant, but he refused to answer on the ground that his answer might incriminate him. He was forced to answer and the Supreme Court upheld the lower court holding that the privilege of refusing to answer an incriminating question is personal to the witness, and can be claimed by him only.

In *State* v. *Simpson,* 133 N. C. 676 (1903), defendant was convicted of fornication and adultery. He appealed to the Supreme Court on the ground that evidence had been improperly admitted. The Court affirmed the judgment and held that when a defendant in a prosecution for another crime, testified in his own behalf, after having been informed of his privilege not to testify, admissions made by him are competent evidence against him in a subsequent trial.

This case should be distinguished from the case of *State* v. *Parker,* 132 N. C. 1014 (1908), where defendant was convicted of carnal knowledge and the Supreme Court ordered a new trial because of the admission of a confession made by the prisoner before a magistrate. The record merely stated that the prisoner was cautioned and the Court held that the trial judge should have found as a fact whether the proper caution was given. In the Simpson case it is stated that the defendant, "being duly sworn, testified," etc. It also appears that he was represented by counsel and that he was expressly notified that he need not testify to incriminating facts.

In *State* v. *Thompson,* 161 N. C. 238 (1912), defendant was convicted of murder in the first degree and appealed. The following evidence was held to be admissible. A state's witness testified in regard to tracks found outside the window and to following them to the house of the prisoner. He stated that when the coroner's jury was at the house of the deceased, the prisoner went to the house with his gun and was put in the tracks, and that the prisoner was of sufficient height to have fired the gun. He was then asked, "Tell how the prisoner acted in taking these measurements," to which the witness answered: "I like not to have got him up there. He did not want to go there at all."

"Q. What did he do? A. Some one handed me a gun. I took him around to the window and handed him the gun. I said, 'Sam, get up; I want to see if you are high enough to do the shooting!' I said, 'You must take the gun.' He did and stepped up and put the gun over his shoulder. I said, 'Put it to the shoulder just like you were going to shoot it.' He fetched the gun up and did like this (witness crouches down). He put his feet within 3 or 4 inches of the track. I said, 'Measure it and put your gun up there.' The gun looked like it might have been that distance, about 7 inches from the window."

"Q. State to the jury, after he put it on his shoulder and pointed, if you got behind and sighted to see where it sighted with reference to where the deceased was sitting. A. It was on a line and the shot was on the line."

The Court observed that the testimony of the constable giving the result of his observation of the prisoner standing at the window and pointing his gun in the direction in which it was known that the deceased was at the time he was shot, is a physical condition as to which he could testify as in the case of the comparison of shoes and footprints.

In this same case the Court held that the testimony comparing the tracks found where a crime had been committed with the shoes worn by the accused does not deprive him of his privilege against self-incrimination guaranteed by the Constitution Article I, Section 11.

In *State* v. *Neville,* 175 N. C. 731 (1918), defendant was convicted of rape and the case was affirmed on appeal. The Court held that testimony that the defendant was placed for identification in the same relative position to a witness as the perpetrator was seen by her just before committing a criminal offense was not objectionable as forcing the defendant to give evidence against himself in denial of his constitutional rights; and the fact that the witness was not so certain of the identity on the day the crime was committed goes only to her credibility, which is for the determination of the jury.

In *State* v. *Mallet,* 125 N. C. 718 (1899), on an indictment for conspiracy to cheat, etc., the sheriff having seized by attachment the ledger and counter-book of the defendants, the Court held that there was no error in using defendant's own entries therein as evidence on the trial.

In the early case of *State* v. *Ellis,* 97 N. C. 447 (1887), it was held that the defendant in a criminal action can only be examined as a witness at his own request; but if he does make such request and is examined, his statement can be held as evidence against him. In *State* v. *Atwood,* 176 N. C. 704 (1918), it was held that when the defendant went on the stand in his own behalf he appeared before the jury both as a witness and as a defendant, and in *State* v. *Cloninger,* 149 N. C. 567 (1908), it was held that he was subject to cross examination. Finally in *State* v. *Simonds,* 154 N. C. 197 (1910), it was held that he waives the privilege not to answer questions which tend to criminate him.

It would be interesting to compare the constitutional provisions and Court decisions with regard to self-incriminating evidence in North Carolina with those of other states, but such a comparison does not properly come within the scope of this study. From a more or less casual reading of the cases it appears that the Court has limited rather than extended the actual wording of the Constitution. Broad general statements have been restricted both by statute and judicial interpretation so that if the defendant elects to go on the stand in his own behalf he may be required to give evidence which is really self-incriminating.

CONFESSIONS

A number of reversals grew out of the improper admission of confessions in evidence. There is a long line of decisions in this state holding that a confession to be admissible must be voluntary and must not be induced by either hope or fear. Most of the errors have occurred in determining when the confession was voluntary and when it was induced by hope or fear, so as to make it admissible in the evidence. It is sometimes a very difficult matter to decide whether the statement of the arresting officer either directly or indirectly induced a confession. But where it was apparent that the confession was induced, the Supreme Court has invariably excluded it from the evidence. The following cases show something of the attitude of the Supreme Court in this regard:

In *State* v. *Drake,* 113 N. C. 624 (1893), defendant was charged with burglary. While the officer was conveying him to the preliminary trial he said to the prisoner: "If you are guilty, I would advise you to make an honest confession. It might be easier for you. It is plain against you"; the prisoner said, "I am not guilty"; and after the preliminary investigation, and while being conducted to the jail by the same officer (who had not withdrawn the inducement to confess which he had held out to the prisoner while on the way to the Magistrate's office), the prisoner made a confession. On appeal the Court held that such a confession was inadmissible as evidence on the trial, since it might have proceeded from the inducement held out to him by the officer when on the way to the Magistrate's office, and if so that there was no guarantee of its truth, and it should have been rejected. So a new trial was accordingly granted.

In *State* v. *Davis,* 125 N. C. 612 (1899), defendant was convicted of larceny in the lower court. The arresting officer testified that he offered no inducements nor made any threats to the prisoner, but that he did tell him he had worked up the case and he had as well tell all about it. At first he denied the charge but after awhile he did confess. On appeal the admission of the confession in the evidence was held to be a reversible error. The Court said, "A confession to be admissible must be freely and voluntarily made; if obtained by operating on the hopes or fears of the prisoner, it is inadmissible."

In the following cases which are more or less representative, confessions were held to be admissible:

In *State* v. *Harrison,* 115 N. C. 706 (1894), defendant was convicted of murder. He appealed on the ground that a confession had been improperly admitted as evidence in the trial. In affirming the lower court's judgment the Supreme Court said, "When a prisoner is advised to tell nothing but the truth, or when what is said to him has no tendency to induce him to make an untrue statement, his confession, in either case is admissible, whether made to an officer or a private individual."

In *State* v. *De Graff,* 113 N. C. 689 (1893), defendant was convicted of murder. On appeal the Court held that the fact that the officer pointed his pistol at the accused to effect his arrest, advising him to give up, did not render incompetent subsequent admissions, especially when no threats or promises were made to induce them and the conduct of the prisoner showed that he had no actual fear of violence.

In *State* v. *Rogers,* 112 N. C. 874 (1893), defendant was

convicted of murder. In affirming the conviction the Court held that the fact that the prisoner was kept tied during his examination before the justice does not of itself constitute a valid objection to the admission of a confession made under the magistrate, unless it appears that he was tied so as to produce pain or to induce or extort from him such confession.

In *State* v. *Jones,* 145 N. C. 466 (1907), defendant was convicted of killing his wife. On appeal it was held that confessions made by the defendant to an officer arresting him, without threat or inducement, that he had killed deceased and knew he was going to hang for it, being voluntary, are competent evidence upon a trial for murder.

In *State* v. *Peterson,* 149 N. C. 533 (1908), the Court held that in a trial for murder where a witness testified that he had said to the accused, "I guess you had him to kill," and the accused answered, "Yes," accused's answer was admissible to prove homicide.

In *State* v. *Drakeford,* 162 N. C. 667 (1913), it was held that statements made by the accused to an officer are not rendered incompetent merely because accused was in jail at the time, unless made under duress or inducements held out to the accused.[3]

CODEFENDANTS

The right of the state to call on one defendant as a witness against a codefendant has occasioned a good deal of discussion in time past, and both the statute and the decisions of the Court have undergone a change. In the early case of *State* v. *Krider,* 78 N. C. 481 (1878), defendants were charged with and convicted of stealing fish. On appeal the Supreme Court reversed the judgment on the ground of a defective

[3] Other cases on this point are: *State* v. *Exum,* 138 N. C. 599 (1905) ; *State* v. *Horner,* 139 N. C. 603 (1905) ; *State* v. *Bonham,* 142 N. C. 695 (1906).

indictment. Faircloth, J., however, delivered the following dictum with regard to the evidence of codefendants in this case: "But it appears from the record that there are two defendants, and that a true bill was obtained by examining each one before the grand jury against the other. We will call the attention of solicitors and the profession to the question whether there is any authority for such practice. At present we are aware of none. It probably arose from a loose construction of the Act of 1866 on the law of evidence. It is objectionable and in the absence of positive statutory enactment cannot be permitted."

But after the *Krider* case the statute was amended and modified a number of times. So in *State v. Smith,* 86 N. C. 705 (1882), Ashe, J., reviewed the act with the several amendments thereto, and held that one defendant is competent and compellable to testify for or against a codefendant, provided his testimony does not criminate himself.

In *State v. Frizell,* 111 N. C. 722 (1892), defendants were indicted for an affray and convicted. The defendants were sent before the grand jury as witnesses against each other. For this reason a motion to quash was made but was denied by the trial judge. On appeal the decision was affirmed and the Court said, "The practice of sending codefendants to the grand jury against each other, while allowed is not commended. They may be compelled to so testify unless the evidence tends to criminate themselves."

In *State v. Collins,* 121 N. C. 667 (1897), larceny being charged, the Supreme Court held that declarations of one of two defendants jointly on trial for larceny are admissible only as against the party making them, and if admitted, it is error not to instruct the jury that such declarations are incompetent as to the other defendants.

The law of the *Smith* case is still the law of the Court in this state. A mere enumeration of the cases and the holdings of the Court in each case would add little or nothing to the treatment of this subject. Minor changes have occurred from time to time, but none of them has been of a fundamental character. It does seem, however, that in a general way the trial judge has assumed a wider discretion in ruling when the witness shall and when he shall not testify, and the Supreme Court has commended this attitude. This point is very well discussed in the case of *State* v. *Medley,* 178 N. C. 710 (1919).

COLLATERAL OFFENSES

There are no specific statutory provisions in this State governing the admission in evidence of the proof that the defendant has committed other offenses of a similar nature. However, the question has often been before the court and the law is well established by judicial precedent.

In *State* v. *Jeffries,* 117 N. C. 727 (1895), defendant was convicted of disposing of mortgaged property. On appeal a new trial was awarded because of the erroneous admission of certain evidence. The Court held that it is only when transactions are so connected or contemporaneous as to form a continuing action that evidence of a distinct and substantive collateral offense will be admitted to prove the intent with which the offense charged was committed; hence, on a trial of one charged with unlawfully disposing of an article of personal property covered by a chattel mortgage with intent to defeat the right of the mortgagee, evidence that, five months after the offense was committed, the defendant offered to dispose of another article covered by the same mortgage is inadmissible to prove the intent with which the offense was committed.

In *State* v. *Frazier,* 118 N. C. 1257 (1896), it was said by the Court that it is a rule of evidence, subject to few exceptions, that evidence of a distinct substantive offense can not be admitted in support of a charge of another offense; therefore, on a charge of larceny of money given to the prosecutrix by the defendant it was error to admit evidence that the defendant had seduced her under promise of marriage, such evidence not showing that he had been compelled to give her the money on account of the seduction. Nor in such case was evidence admissible as to defendant's inability (he being a married man) to make good his promise of marriage.

In *State* v. *Graham,* 121 N. C. 623 (1897), defendant was convicted of arson. On appeal a new trial was ordered because evidence was admitted that the defendant at a prior time was guilty of a similar offense. The Court held that it is only when the transactions are so connected or contemporaneous as to form a continuing action that evidence of a collateral offense will be heard to prove the intent of the offense charged.

In *State* v. *Fowler,* 172 N. C. 905 (1916), defendant was convicted of housebreaking and robbery. On appeal a new trial was ordered because of the admission of collateral evidence. The Court held that where the indictment charges the defendant with breaking into a building and stealing a certain sum of money therefrom, it is a reversible error for the court to admit over the defendant's objection testimony that other buildings had been broken into and other thefts therein committed, when there is no evidence that the defendant committed any of the other crimes or had anything to do with them.

In *State* v. *Beam,* 179 N. C. 768 (1920), it was held that where there was evidence that the defendant had liquor in his possession for the purpose of sale, in violation of the statute, evidence that he had liquor in his possession and had sold the same a year previous in another county, is not so connected with or related to the offense charged as to be competent to show the intent or guilty knowledge in committing the same, nor is it within the reason of the rule which admits evidence of collateral crimes to prove motive or intent. Accordingly a new trial was ordered.

In the following cases the action of the lower court was affirmed on appeal to the Supreme Court. There are other cases, but those given below are perhaps sufficiently expressive of the principles of law to serve as an illustration.

In *State* v. *Mace,* 118 N. C. 1244 (1896), in a murder trial, it was held that while it is a general rule that when a prisoner is on trial for one crime, evidence of his commission of other crimes will not be admitted; still other criminal acts may be proved if they are connected with the one charged.

In *State* v. *Smarr,* 121 N. C. 669 (1897), defendant was convicted of burglary in the first degree and sentenced to be hanged. In affirming the judgment of the lower court the Supreme Court said, "In the trial of a person for burglary it is not competent for him to show that other burglaries were committed in the same neighborhood about the same time as the one with which he is charged, was committed."

In the older case of *State* v. *Murphey,* 84 N. C. 742 (1881), defendant was convicted of larceny. The decision was affirmed on appeal. The Court held that evidence of a collateral offense of the same character and connected with that charged in an indictment, and tending to prove the guilty knowledge of the defendant, when that is an essential element of the crime, is admissible; therefore on the trial of an indictment for the larceny of a hog, where the prosecutor testified that he identified the property as his, in an enclosure of the defendant and demanded its delivery to him, it was competent for the state to prove by the testimony of another witness that, at the same time and place and in the presence of the prosecutor and defendant, such witness said that the other hog therein was his, and he then and there claimed and demanded it of defendant.

From a review of the cases the law seems to be that when offenses are so connected with, or related to, each other that the commission of one tends to show the intent with which the other was committed, it becomes competent to introduce evidence of the commission of an offense of the same sort as that being investigated, for the purpose of showing intent; but when the crimes are wholly independent of each other, even though they are crimes of the same kind, such evidence being irrelevant, is inadmissible.

CHARACTER

The admission or exclusion of certain evidence with regard to character has been responsible for a number of reversals in the Supreme Court. By the Act of 1881, Chapter 110 (*Code,* sec 1353), defendant was given the right and privilege in all criminal indictments, complaints and other proceedings, at his own request, but not otherwise to be a competent witness. Before the passage of the Act the state could not impeach the character of a defendant unless the defendant himself opened the way by offering through the testimony of witnesses evidence of his general character.

The first case in which the statute of 1881 was discussed was *State* v. *Efler,* 85 N. C. 585 (1881). In this case the defendant was examined in his own behalf and the state, for the purpose of discrediting him as a witness and for no other purpose, offered testimony of his general bad character, and it was admitted by the court below for that purpose alone. The Court said in declaring him to be a competent witness, "We understand the statute to mean that he shall occupy the same position with any other witness, be under obligation to tell the truth, entitled to the same privileges, receive the same protection and equally likely to be impeached or discredited. . . . But by availing himself of the statute he assumes the position of a witness and subjects himself to all the disadvantages of that position, and his credibility is to be weighed and tested as that of any other witness."

In *State* v. *Hice,* 117 N. C. 782 (1895), defendants were convicted of fornication and adultery. In the trial neither of the defendants testified in their own behalf but did introduce a witness to show good character. The court sustained an objection to admitting this evidence and defendants appealed. This exclusion was held to be an error and the Court added that in all cases a person accused of a felony or misdemeanor, may, on the trial, offer testimony of his good character and that this right does not depend upon the defendant's having been examined as a witness in his own behalf. But in case a defendant offers testimony as to his good character, the prosecution may show defendant's bad character either by cross-examination or by other witnesses.

In *State* v. *Traylor,* 121 N. C. 674 (1897), defendant was indicted for forgery of a promissory bank note and convicted. Defendant testified during the trial in his own behalf but introduced no evidence as to his general character, but the state introduced evidence to show that his character was bad. It was held on appeal that such evidence by the state could be considered only as affecting the credibility of the defendant as a witness and not as a circumstance in determining the question of his guilt or innocence, so a new trial was granted.

In *State* v. *Spurling,* 118 N. C. 1250 (1896), defendant was convicted of slandering an innocent and virtuous woman. Upon appeal a new trial was ordered because certain evidence was excluded with regard to the character of the prosecutrix. A state's witness testified that the prosecutrix's character was good up to the time the trouble began. On cross-examination, this witness was asked by defendant's counsel: "What is her character now?" The state objected and the objection was sustained. The Court held that when a prosecutor or defendant in a criminal action goes upon the stand as a witness, he becomes just as any other witness, and his general character can be proven, not only as it was before a charge affecting it was made, but as it is at the date he goes upon the stand.

In *State* v. *Foster,* 130 N. C. 666 (1902), defendant was charged with, and convicted of murder in the first degree. The defendant had gone on the stand as a witness in his own behalf but introduced no evidence as to his character. The state placed a witness on the stand who testified that the defendant had the reputation of being a "little fussy." On appeal the Supreme Court held that this evidence was inadmissible since the defendant had not put his character in question.

In *State* v. *Cloninger,* 149 N. C. 576 (1908), defendants were convicted of manslaughter. In this case the conviction was affirmed on appeal and the Court held that for the sole purpose of contradicting his testimony, it was competent for the state to cross-examine a defendant, a witness in his own behalf, on a trial for murder, when he has introduced no evidence as to his character; and the cross-examination is not restricted to matters brought out on the direct examination. *Revisal,* sec. 1634.

In *State* v. *Atwood,* 176 N. C. 704 (1918), defendant was

indicted and convicted of murder in the second degree. In affirming the judgment of the lower court it was held that when a prisoner, accused of homicide, testifies to a matter in justification or to disprove inferences to be drawn from the evidence against him, he puts his character at issue, both as a witness and as a defendant, and the jury may consider the evidence of character as substantive evidence whether he would or would not commit a crime of the kind charged.

In this same case it was held that when a witness, charged with a crime, has taken the stand in his own behalf, and the state has introduced evidence of his bad character, he may not complain that it was not restricted to his character as a witness, unless he has asked at the time of the admission that it be so restricted. Supreme Court Rule Number 27.

It was further held in the same case that a prisoner charged with a crime, and who has testified in his own behalf, may not put on evidence in rebuttal of that of the state tending to show his bad character, and have it confined to his credibility as a witness.

HUSBAND OR WIFE AS A WITNESS

At common law, the husband or wife of a party to a suit was an incompetent witness either for or against the other, except in criminal action against one of them for personal injury to the other. They were also incompetent to testify to communications with each other, as to any fact or transaction, the knowledge of which was obtained by means of the marital relation.[5]

But the common-law rule was changed by the statutes of 1868-69, c. 209, and 1881, c. 110. The statute is now Section 1802 of the *Consolidated Statutes* and is as follows:

[5] T. W. Hughes, *On Evidence,* p. 278 (Chicago, 1907).

The husband or wife of the defendant, in all criminal actions or proceedings shall be a competent witness for the defendant, but the failure of such a witness to be examined shall not be used to the prejudice of the defense. Every such person examined as a witness shall be subject to be cross-examined as are other witnesses. No husband or wife shall be compellable to disclose any confidential communication made by one to the other during their marriage. Nothing herein shall render any husband or wife competent or compellable to give evidence against each other in any criminal action or proceding, except to prove the fact of marriage in case of bigamy, and except that in all criminal prosecutions of a husband for an assault and battery upon his wife, or for abandoning his wife, or for neglecting to provide for her support, it shall be lawful to examine the wife in behalf of the state against the husband.

The following cases show some of the problems that have grown out of the above statutes and the construction placed upon them by the Court:

In *State* v. *Brittain,* 117 N. C. 783 (1895), defendants were convicted of incest and appealed. The Court held that the general rule that evidence competent against only one of several defendants is admissible with instructions by the court that it shall not be considered as against the other, is subject to the exception that a confidential communication between husband and wife can not, on grounds of public policy, be so admitted as evidence. In the same case it was held that where a wife, on threats of her husband to leave her, confessed to having committed incest, such confession being a confidential communication is inadmissible and its subsequent repetition to a third party under similar circumstances, in the presence of the husband, is incompetent in the trial of an indictment against the wife and another for incest, so a new trial was awarded for the improper admission of such evidence.

In *State* v. *Raby,* 121 N. C. 682 (1897), defendant was tried and convicted on a charge of fornication and adultery. On appeal a new trial was granted. It was held that under Section 588 of *The Code,* a divorced husband is incompetent to testify against the divorced wife in the trial of an indictment against her for fornication and adultery which occurred prior to the divorce.

In *State* v. *Wallace,* 162 N. C. 623 (1913), defendant was convicted of the larceny of $1,650 in money. Appeal was taken on the ground that a certain letter had been improperly admitted in the evidence. The Court held that upon the trial of a husband for a criminal offense, it is competent for a third person as a witness to introduce in evidence a letter written by the prisoner to his wife relevant and pertinent upon the question of his guilt, and procured without the consent or privity of the wife; and that such evidence is not against the policy of the common law that the wife should not be permitted to testify or offer in evidence communications to her from her husband with incriminating effect upon the latter. The Court further held that the unlawful procurement by searching his home in his absence, of a letter pertinent and relevant to the prisoner's guilt upon the charge of a criminal offense, will not affect its introduction in evidence upon the trial.

In the case of *State* v. *McDuffee,* 107 N. C. 885 (1890), defendant was indicted for fornication and adultery. It was held that the first wife of the defendant is a competent witness to prove the marriage; public cohabitation as man and wife being public acknowledgements of the relation and not coming within the nature of confidential relations which the policy of the law forbids either to give evidence.

In *State* v. *Chester,* 172 N. C. 946 (1916), in a trial for abandonment, it was held that the wife is competent to prove the fact of marriage under an indictment against her husband for abandonment, *Revisal,* section 1635; and construing this section with 1636, it was held that by allowing, under the latter section, the wife to prove such a fact under indictments for bigamy, and in actions or proceedings for divorce on account of adultery, it was not the legislative intent that such testimony be excluded upon trial for abandonment, and that these two sections are not in conflict with each other.

The case of *State* v. *Alderman,* 182 N. C. 917 (1921), is a novel one and deserves special consideration. Here the defendants were convicted on four counts of poisoning a husband and father. On appeal the conviction was sustained. The Court held that in case of an assault and battery with intent to kill by poison, with evidence tending to show the previous threats of the wife, and that the poison was put into the food prepared by the daughter in her mother's presence at their home, and that the husband was poisoned by eating thereof, the testimony of the husband as to the wife's previous threats is not inadmissible under the provisions of the *Consolidated Statutes,* Section 1802, but is admissible for the purpose of showing knowledge and identifying the perpetrators of the crime, and is distinguishable from the rule that threats are ordinarily inadmissible in trials for assault and battery.

It is a difficult matter to follow the logic of this decision. Upon the general principles of common law the husband was an incompetent witness for or against his wife. The statute referred to by the Court does make the wife a competent witness in behalf of the state against her husband in certain matters, but the husband is not empowered to testify against his wife. The Court could not have been inadvertent to the statute in general since specific mention is made of it. Apparently the Court in construing this statute held that since the wife in assault and battery cases may in some instances testify as to the previous threats of the husband,

a similar right of testifying against the wife may also
be extended to the husband. This decision seems to be
a departure from the course usually followed since the
Court gave the husband the right to testify, which right
is given neither by common law nor by this statute.

Newly Discovered Testimony

The statute of 1815, c. 895, provided that the courts
might grant new trials in criminal cases when the defendant is found guilty, under the same rules and
regulations as in civil cases. In the early case of *State
v. Starnes,* 97 N. C. 423 (1887), rape being charged,
Smith, C. J., speaking for the Court said in part:

When this case was before the Court on the former appeal of the defendant, 94 N. C. 937, and no error was found
in the record of which the prisoner could complain, application for an order for a new trial to be had in the court
below was made upon the ground of the discovery of new
material testimony in favor of the accused, since the former
trial. The motion, so far as our own and the researches of
counsel disclose, is without precedent in the administration
of criminal law on appeals to this Court, and so funda-
mentally repugnant to the functions of a reviewing Court,
whose office is to examine and determine assigned errors
appearing in the record, that we did not look into the affi-
davits offered in support of the motion, nor hesitate in
denying it.

In *State v. DeGraff,* 113 N. C. 688 (1893), defendant
was convicted of murder. The judgment of the lower court
was affirmed on appeal. It was held that the granting of
a new trial upon newly discovered evidence is, in the absence of gross abuse, within the discretion of the trial judge,
and a refusal to exercise such discretion is not reviewable
upon appeal. Such discretion will not be exercised where
the new testimony is merely cumulative or only tends to

contradict or discredit the opposing witness; hence, where the newly discovered evidence upon which a new trial was asked by the prisoner was that a witness for the state had, before the trial, spoken in hostile terms of the prisoner and wished for his conviction, the discretion of the judge was properly exercised by refusing the motion.

In *State* v. *Arthur*, 151 N. C. 653 (1909), defendant was convicted of house burning. In refusing a motion for a new trial the Court said in substance that no case in this country had been cited where a new trial had been allowed in criminal cases by an appellate court upon the ground of newly discovered evidence, and it is not allowed in Great Britain. If such practice prevailed, the proper administration of criminal law in which our entire people are interested, would be seriously impaired and the delays incident to it greatly increased.

In *State* v. *Trull*, 169 N. C. 363 (1915), it was held that the findings of the trial judge upon a motion before him for a new trial upon newly discovered evidence, and his refusal of the motion, are not reviewable upon appeal.

From the above cases it is evident that a new trial will not be granted by the Supreme Court in a criminal offense for newly discovered evidence. There may be cases where this rule works a hardship on the defendant, but generally speaking it seems to be a good rule.

INSUFFICIENT EVIDENCE

Table VI shows a reversal of thirty cases because the evidence was insufficient to convict or to support the verdict. Apparently most of the errors were due to an improper evaluation of the weight of testimony submitted. It is possible in this state to convict even of murder in the first degree upon circumstantial evidence.[6] Where a good deal of weight is given to the

[6] *State* v. *Vaughan*, 129 N. C. 502 (1901).

value of circumstantial evidence, it is an easy matter to jump to a conclusion of guilt when in reality the evidence may not substantiate such conclusion beyond a reasonable doubt as required by law.[7] The law with regard to sufficiency of evidence is pretty well summarized in *State* v. *Kiger,* 115 N. C. 746 (1894). Here it was held that where there is no sufficient evidence to permit a case to go to the jury, the trial judge may so rule and withdraw the case from the jury; but if the evidence is merely weak and such as would not induce the judge, if a juror, to convict, he has no authority so to withdraw the case. In the same case it was held that the trial judge is vested with the power to set aside a verdict and grant a new trial if he deems the verdict to be against the evidence or the evidence insufficient to justify conviction; but as this is a matter of discretion, his granting or refusing a new trial on such grounds, is not reviewable.

We shall now consider a few illustrative cases which were reversed because the evidence was held to be insufficient.

In *State* v. *Goodson,* 107 N. C. 798 (1890), defendant was convicted of murder. The evidence tended to show that the deceased, a woman, was found dead just outside her house, near the town of Marion. The body bore evidence of a brutal murder and an attempt to burn. The prisoner, who was a laborer on a railroad nearby, and had been seen frequently, previous to the murder, going in the direction of the deceased's house, and, on the afternoon of the day preceding the finding of the body, was seen talking with a person who resided near deceased, after which he went in the direction of her house. Shortly after, he was seen in the town, drinking. He spoke of going to see his

[7] *State* v. *Wilcox,* 132 N. C. 1120 (1903).

"old gal," etc. He was further heard to say: "I expect to kill some d—d woman, and have got enough money to carry me wherever I want to go." A witness said he saw a person he believed to be the prisoner, on the same afternoon, going as if from the house of the deceased, across a field, not in any pathway, and he was walking briskly— "almost in a trot"—and, once or twice without stopping, looked back toward the deceased's house. After his arrest the prisoner's clothing was examined, and splotches, which had the appearance of blood, were found upon it; but the tracks near the place of the homicide, did not correspond with the prisoner's foot. The prisoner made no attempt to fly. On appeal the Supreme Court held that while these facts established a strong suspicion against the prisoner, they were not sufficient to warrant his conviction of murder. . . . A new trial was ordered.

In *State* v. *Pope,* 109 N. C. 849 (1891), defendants were convicted of fornication and adultery. There was evidence that they lived in the house of the male defendant for some time, but occupied different rooms; that the female defendant washed, cooked and performed other housekeeping duties but there was no real evidence of improper relations and the conviction of the lower court was held to be erroneous for insufficient evidence.

In *State* v. *Davis,* 126 N. C. 1059 (1900), defendants were convicted of disturbing religious worship. This decision was held to be erroneous because the state's evidence that the services (held at night) had been concluded for ten minutes, the lights were out, and the congregation had dispersed before the disturbance occurred, was insufficient to justify such conviction.

In 1913 a law was passed which gives the defendant the right to move for a judgment of nonsuit after the state's evidence is completed, and, if the motion is granted, it has the same force as a judgment of not guilty. If there is really no evidence the trial is thus shortened. On the other hand, if the motion is refused, the defendant may introduce other evidence and make a similar motion when all the evidence has been submitted. If the motion is not granted it is a ground for noting an exception.[8]

In *State* v. *Bradshaw,* 182 N. C. 769 (1921), defendant was convicted of having engaged in immoral prostitution and unlawfully using a building for like purpose in violation of *Consolidated Statutes,* Section 4357 *et seq.* The judgment was reversed for lack of evidence to justify the verdict and it was held that the motion for judgment as of nonsuit should have been granted under *Laws of 1913,* c. 73.

[8] When on the trial of any criminal action in the Superior Court, or any criminal court, the state has produced its evidence and rested its case, the defendant may move to dismiss the action or for judgment of nonsuit. If the motion is allowed, judgment shall be entered accordingly; and such judgment shall have the force and effect of a verdict of "not guilty" as to such defendant. If the motion is refused, the defendant may except; and if the defendant introduces no evidence, the case shall be submitted to the jury as in other cases, and the defendant shall have the benefit of his exception on appeal to the Supreme Court.

Nothing in this section shall prevent the defendant from introducing evidence after his motion for nonsuit has been overruled; and he may again move for a judgment of nonsuit after all the evidence in the case is concluded. If the motion is thus refused, upon the consideration of all the evidence, the defendant may except; and after the jury has rendered its verdict, he shall have the benefit of such latter exception on appeal to the Supreme Court. If the defendant's motion for judgment of nonsuit be granted, or be sustained on appeal to the Supreme Court, it shall in all cases have the force and effect of a verdict of "not guilty." *Consolidated Statutes,* sec. 4643; 1913, c. 73; *Ex. Sess. 1913,* c. 32.

In *State* v. *Everett,* 194 N. C. 442 (1927), upon a conviction of manslaughter the defendant appealed to the Supreme Court which reversed the decision because the evidence tended only to show that the prisoner unintentionally in his sleep as a result of a bad dream, inflicted upon his wife a wound too slight to have caused her death except that from neglect, etc., blood poison might have set in and caused her death. This evidence was insufficient to sustain the conviction.

CHAPTER VIII

ERROR IN THE FORM OF THE VERDICT

TABLE VI[1] shows nineteen reversals because defective verdicts were returned by the jury. Where the system of special verdicts is as widely used as it has been in this state, there is likely to be some confusion on the matter till the law and practice are really clarified. We shall consider a few cases where the verdicts have been held to be defective.

ILLUSTRATIVE CASES

In *State* v. *Moore,* 107 N. C. 770 (1890), violation of a city ordinance being charged and a finding on a special verdict of not guilty the state appealed. The Court held that a special verdict which simply finds a certain state of facts, without a formal verdict of guilty or not guilty, in accordance with the opinion of the court given upon the facts found, is incomplete and will not support a judgment.

In *State* v. *Neis,* 107 N. C. 820 (1890), when the jury returned a certain state of facts, and a verdict thereon, "guilty or not guilty, as the court may be of the opinion as to the law," and the court assumed to pass judgment without directing a verdict to be entered up in accordance with its opinion on the law, there was held to be an error and that a verdict must be absolute and unconditional.

In *State* v. *Hight,* 124 N. C. 845 (1899), an indictment charged an assault with intent to commit a rape, and also a simple assault, so a general verdict of guilty was held to apply to both counts. When there was no evidence applicable to the count for the assault with intent, etc. and the jury were properly so instructed, a general verdict of guilty was erroneous, and so was a judgment imposing a longer term of imprisonment than is allowed for simple assault.

[1] See *supra,* p. 33.

In *State* v. *Truesdale,* 125 N. C. 696 (1899), in an indictment and conviction for murder, the defendant appealed. It was held that under the Act of 1893, Chapter 85, distinguishing murder in two degrees, the jury on conviction, must determine in their verdict whether the crime is murder in the *first* or *second* degree, and the record must show that they have so done in order that there may be a proper judgment. When the transcript of the record says the verdict was, that the prisoner "was guilty of the felony and murder in manner and form as charged in the bill of indictment," and the statement of the case on appeal says "a verdict of murder in the first degree was rendered by the jury," a new trial will be granted.

In *State* v. *McCloud,* 151 N. C. 730 (1909), upon a special verdict the defendant was adjudged not guilty and the state appealed. The special verdict was held to be defective as it did not find the intent with which defendant made certain statements. The Court held that "the *intent* to cheat and defraud the prosecutor was an essential ingredient in the crime of false pretense and that the verdict should have found that fact distinctly, the one way or the other; either that the defendant made the false representation with intent to cheat, or that he made the statement under an honest conviction of its truth, etc."

In *State* v. *Spear,* 164 N. C. 452 (1913), on an indictment for burglary, the jury rendered the following verdict: "We, the jury, find the defendant guilty of housebreaking, with no intent to commit a felony. The jury especially ask the mercy of the court." From a conviction of burglarious breaking the defendant appealed and it was held that the verdict was equivalent to an acquittal and that the judgment of not guilty should have been entered by the court and defendant discharged.

In *State* v. *Fenner,* 166 N. C. 247 (1914), defendant was charged with the crime against nature and convicted. On appeal it was held that a verdict which contained merely a recital of evidence of a circumstantial nature was defective and would not support a judgment.

GENERAL PRINCIPLES APPLYING TO VERDICTS

Whatever may have been the situation in the past we have reason to expect fewer and fewer errors in the future with regard to the form and substance of verdicts. After all, a great deal depends on the judge himself, and, if he is vigilant, he can prevent the return of a defective verdict from the jury in most cases. In the case of *State* v. *Snipes,* 185 N. C. 743 (1923), Mr. Justice Adams speaking for the Court set forth the following principles which are generally recognized and applied in this state with regard to verdicts:

1. A verdict must be certain and responsive to the issue or issues submitted to the court.

2. While a change merely as to form is not fatal, the court can not amend or change a verdict in any matter of substance without the consent of the jury, and can not do so with their consent after the verdict has been finally accepted and recorded; but if the verdict is responsive to the issue or issues submitted, and is otherwise sufficient, additional words which are not a part of the legal verdict may be treated as surplusage. . . .

3. Where the indictment contains several counts and the evidence applies to one or more, but not to all, a general verdict will be presumed to have been returned on the count or counts to which the evidence relates.

4. When the indictment contains several counts and there is a verdict of guilty as to some but no verdict as to others, the failure to return a verdict as to the latter is equivalent to a verdict of not guilty.

5. If a verdict as returned is not complete, but is ambiguous in its terms, the ambiguity may sometimes be explained and the verdict construed by reference to and in connection with the evidence and the charge of the court.

JUDGMENT ON SPECIAL VERDICT

Consolidated Statutes, 585, defines a general verdict as being "that by which the jury pronounce generally upon all or any of the issues, either in favor of the plaintiff or the defendant." The same section defines a special verdict as "one by which the jury finds the facts only, leaving the judgment to the court." During the period under consideration forty-seven cases were reversed because of an improper judgment on the special verdict. It is interesting to note that in the great majority of these cases the defendant was charged with a mere misdemeanor, such as retailing without license, fornication and adultery and forcible trespass. We do not think that a discussion of these cases is necessary. Suffice it to say that wherever possible special verdicts should be avoided. If they are used great care should be taken to see that they are sufficient in form and substance and adequate in scope.

CHAPTER IX

UNCONSTITUTIONAL ORDINANCES AND LAWS

ILLUSTRATIVE CASES

TABLE VI[1] shows that fourteen cases were reversed because the indictment was brought for the violation of an invalid ordinance law, or because the lower court had held invalid some ordinance or law which was valid. The invalid (or supposedly invalid) statutes range in importance from a minor city ordinance infringing the police power to a violation of the Constitution of the United States. We shall consider a few cases which will indicate something of the nature of the problems before the Court for adjudication.

In *State* v. *Taft,* 118 N. C. 1190 (1896), defendant was charged with violating a town ordinance which forbade the importation and sale of second-hand clothing in the town of Louisburg. He was convicted before the Mayor and on appeal to the Superior Court the action was affirmed. The Supreme Court held that the ordinance was unreasonable, and that the commissioners transcended their powers in passing it, since it prohibits a business lawful in itself and not necessarily dangerous.

In *State* v. *Thomas,* 118 N. C. 1221 (1896), defendant was convicted of violating a city ordinance of Marion, which prohibited keeping open barrooms between the hours of 10 P.M. and 4 o'clock A.M. He appealed to the Supreme Court on the ground that the ordinance was invalid. The decision was reversed because it was held that *The Code,* Section 3799, did not empower a town to pass an ordinance forbidding one who sells liquor to occupy his own premises between certain hours.

[1] See *supra,* p. 33.

In *State* v. *Ray,* 131 N. C. 814 (1902), an ordinance of Scotland Neck requiring stores to be closed after 7:30 in the evening was held invalid.

In *State* v. *Darnell,* 166 N. C. 300 (1914), defendant was convicted of violating an ordinance of Winston, which made it unlawful for any colored person to occupy as a residence any house upon any street or alley between two adjacent streets, on which a greater number of houses were occupied by white than colored people. The ordinance contained a similar limitation with regard to white people. On appeal the Court held that the legislative authority given to a town to pass any ordinance for the good order, good government, or general welfare of the city, provided that it did not conflict with the laws and Constitution of the state, did not contemplate the passage of an ordinance prohibiting the ownership of land in certain localities and districts, by white or colored people, in accordance with whether the majority of the land owners in that district were white or colored people, such being in contravention of the general policy of the State and questionable as to its validity under the Federal Constitution.

In *State* v. *Freshwater,* 183 N. C. 762 (1922), defendant was convicted of violating an ordinance of the town of Burlington limiting the speed of automobiles in the fire district to eight miles per hour. . . . On appeal the Supreme Court held that the ordinance was clearly in conflict with *Consolidated Statutes,* Sections 2599 and 2618, and that the city ordinance must yield to the state law.

JURISDICTION AND VENUE

As shown in Table VI,[2] ten cases were reversed because the court in which the action was brought was without jurisdiction. In several other cases lack of jurisdiction was assigned as an error but the decision seemed to be primarily upon other considerations,

[2] See *supra,* p. 33.

though jurisdiction unquestionably influenced the Court and was used as a flying buttress to support the decision. Most of the cases involving jurisdiction have grown out of statutory provisions which attempted to vest jurisdiction in some particular court or provide a punishment for the offense.

In *State* v. *Fesperman,* 108 N. C. 770 (1891), the indictment charged an assault with a deadly weapon but the proof showed a simple assault. The Superior Court held that it had no jurisdiction in the case. On appeal the Supreme Court held that on an indictment charging an assault with a deadly weapon the Superior Court retained its jurisdiction even though the proof showed only simple assault. The Court added that the Constitution makes the measure of the punishment which a justice of the peace may impose the test of his exclusive jurisdiction in criminal actions; therefore, an act which simply declares that justices of the peace shall have exclusive jurisdiction of certain offenses, without fixing the punishment within the constitutional limit, is inoperative. . . . The case was remanded for further proceedings and sentence.

In *State* v. *Hall,* 114 N. C. 909 (1894), defendants were indicted and convicted of murder (Hall as principal and Dockery as accessory before the fact). From the evidence, it appeared that the deceased was wounded and died in Tennessee, and that the fatal wounds were inflicted by the prisoners shooting the deceased from a point in North Carolina. The real question presented in the case was whether the crime came within the jurisdiction of the courts of this state. Proceedings were begun which were carried to the Supreme Court. The Court followed the statutes 2 and 3 Edward VI and the old common law rule of trial where death occurs, that crime was territorial and that the infliction of the wound was the same in contemplation of the law as if the defendant had followed the shot to the place of death. A new trial was granted because the Court believed that the courts of Tennessee alone had jurisdiction of the case. The fact that both the defendants and the deceased were citizens of North Carolina was held not to give our courts jurisdiction.

The following year a statute was passed to cure the defect of jurisdiction which became apparent in this case:

If any person, being in this state, unlawfully and wilfully puts in motion a force from the effect of which any person is injured while in another state, the person so setting such force in motion shall be guilty of the same offense in this state as he would be if the effect had taken place within this state.[3]

In *State* v. *Glover,* 112 N. C. 896 (1893), the defendant was indicted for embezzlement but pleaded that the court had no jurisdiction and the court sustained his demurrer and ordered his discharge from custody. The state appealed. It appeared that the defendant had been surrendered by the state of Pennsylvania to answer a charge of obtaining money by false pretense. He argued that he could not be tried on the charge of embezzlement until after the trial for the offense upon which he had been extradited, and until he had sufficient time and opportunity to return to the state from which he was extradited. In reviewing the case the Supreme Court held that the Federal case of *U. S.* v. *Rauscher,* 119 U. S. 407 (1886), had no application to interstate rendition, but that the case of *Lascelle* v. *State,* 16 S. E. R. 949 (1892), was controlling and remanded the case to the court below for further proceedings and a proper judgment.

In *State* v. *Baskerville,* 141 N. C. 811 (1906), defendant was convicted and sentenced in a court of justice of the

[3] *Revisal,* sec. 3237 (1895), c. 169; *Consolidated Statutes,* 4604.

peace of Raleigh Township, for violating a valid ordinance of the city, and appealed to the Superior Court, contending that the Justice of the Peace had no jurisdiction to try the case. Defendant moved for dismissal for want of jurisdiction, his motion was overruled, sentence passed and he excepted. The Supreme Court held that the justice of the peace had no jurisdiction in the case, and since the Superior Court had only appellate jurisdiction the case depended on the jurisdiction of the court of the justice of the peace, so judgment was arrested.

In *State* v. *Wilkes,* 149 N. C. 453 (1908), an indictment originated in the Superior Court of Greene County for wilfully abandoning a crop without cause before paying advances, etc. A motion in arrest of judgment because the Superior Court had no original jurisdiction was overruled. On appeal it was held that a Justice of the Peace has final jurisdiction (*Revisal,* section 3366), and so the judgment was arrested.

In *State* v. *McAden,* 162 N. C. 575 (1913), defendant was convicted under Chapter 445, *Laws of 1909,* regulating the use of public highways by motor vehicles. The statute provided that the violation thereof was a mere misdemeanor and should be punished by a fine not exceeding fifty dollars or imprisonment not exceeding twenty days "or both," etc. The words "or both" were held to take the jurisdiction out of the hands of the Justice of the Peace. The case was tried *de novo* in the Superior Court upon an amended warrant without a bill of indictment when as a matter of fact the Justice of the Peace had no jurisdiction and the Superior Court could proceed only upon a true bill of indictment, so the case was reversed.

In *State* v. *Coble,* 181 N. C. 554 (1921), on an indictment for assault with deadly weapons, a Justice of the Peace bound a child under sixteen years of age over to the Superior Court. The defendant saved his right and appealed to the Supreme Court, which ordered the case remanded tc

the Superior Court with orders to dismiss the indictment
and that the defendant be committed to the juvenile court
for further proceedings.[4]

[4] Other cases reversed for want of jurisdiction or improper
venue are: *State* v. *Buchanan,* 130 N. C. 660 1902) ; *State* v.
Patterson, 134 N. C. 612 (1904) ; *State* v. *Lytle,* 138 N. C. 738
(1905).

CHAPTER X

MISCELLANEOUS PROCEDURAL ERRORS

ILLUSTRATIVE CASES

A NUMBER of cases have been carried to the Supreme Court on account of alleged errors or irregularities in the court procedure. We shall give a number of cases where the court held the proceedings to be irregular and erroneous, and a few where there was held to be no prejudicial error, though there was a departure from the usual process.

In *State* v. *Shuford,* 128 N. C. 588 (1901), defendant was convicted of larceny. He appealed to the Supreme Court on the ground that the court which tried him was illegally constituted. It was held that the appointment of a Judge of the Superior Court prior to the date when the act creating the judicial district takes effect was invalid, and a motion in arrest of judgment by a person convicted of larceny, on the ground that the court was illegally constituted, should have been allowed.

In *State* v. *Brown,* 127 N. C. 561 (1900), the Court held that under the *Acts of 1899* c. 593, providing for an extra term of Superior Court without a grand jury, at which only cases against incarcerated defendants should be tried, it was proper to quash an indictment returned by a grand jury at such term, charging defendant, who was in jail, with carrying a concealed weapon, since there could be no legal grand jury, and the extra term could only try criminal cases where indictments had already been found.

In *State* v. *Whisenant,* 149 N. C. 515 (1908), defendant was charged with the unlawful sale of intoxicating liquors and ciders. The trial judge entered a verdict different from that rendered by the jury. This was held to be an error, so the Court reversed the decision and ordered the prisoner discharged.

In *State* v. *Jenkins,* 116 N. C. 972 (1895), defendant was charged with injury to stock running at large. From a verdict and sentence of guilty he appealed to the Supreme Court because the jurors purchased and drank whisky and "some of them were under its influence" while deliberating on their verdict. A new trial was accordingly granted and the former verdict declared null and void.

In *State* v. *Perry,* 121 N. C. 533 (1897), where an indictment charged rape, it was held to be ground for a new trial that the jury visited the scene of the crime, whether with or without leave of the court, interrogated a passer-by as to the identity of the house whose distance from the scene of the crime was material and thus elicited other evidence (unsworn) than that offered on the trial.

In *State* v. *Boggan,* 133 N. C. 761 (1903), in a prosecution for homicide, it was shown on a motion for a new trial that the jury was quartered in a hotel adjoining an alley in which the killing occurred, and that on two occasions the jury were conducted through the alley to the lavatory. In reference to these facts, the court found that while the jury could and did see the circumstances as to the light, etc., surrounding the killing, they made no mention of any such things and did not remark thereon in their deliberations or anywhere else. On appeal it was held that the court's findings would be construed to indicate that the jury were not influenced by what they saw, and the refusal to set the verdict aside would not be disturbed.

In *State* v. *Scruggs,* 115 N. C. 805 (1894), murder being charged, while one of the state's witnesses was testifying one of the jurors was taken ill and excused by the court. Counsel for the defendant proposed to continue with eleven jurors or to select another from the special venire. The solicitor objected and the court ordered a mistrial and a new trial. The Supreme Court, in dismissing the appeal, held that no appeal lies in a criminal action until after the rendition of a final judgment in the case and that the action of the court below was regular and within the sound discretion of the judge.

In *State* v. *Tyson,* 138 N. C. 627 (1905), defendant was charged with the capital felony of murder. At a former term he was placed on trial under the same bill of indictment but the trial judge had ordered a mistrial and discharged the jury on account of the drunken condition of a juror which incapacitated him for further service. Exception was taken to overruling the plea of former jeopardy in the lower court, and in this, the Supreme Court found no error.

In *State* v. *Crowder,* 193 N. C. 130 (1927), defendant was convicted of embezzlement. He moved to quash because the solicitor was in the grand jury room and assisted in finding a true bill against him. The motion was denied and he appealed to the Supreme Court, which reversed the decision as being erroneous.

In *State* v. *Ford,* 168 N. C. 165 (1914), where the judge had ordered an entry to be made by the clerk of a verdict of not guilty on the trial of a criminal case, for a variance between the offense charged in the indictment and the proof, but conceiving his action to be erroneous, he then, in the presence of the jury, still sitting on the case, directed the clerk to strike out the entry and withdrew a juror and directed a mistrial. The Court dismissing the appeal held that the order of the judge striking out the verdict of guilty left the case in exactly the same attitude it was in before the entry of the verdict, and the withdrawal of the juror and the order of mistrial, being in the discretion of the court, except in capital cases, are not reviewable.

In *State* v. *Pierce,* 123 N. C. 745 (1898), defendant was convicted of burning a gin-house. He moved for a new trial on the ground that the court had proceeded with the trial during his temporary absence from the courtroom. The Court held that the temporary absence of the prisoner from the courtroom, during the argument of his counsel, who waived the objection and proceeded with his argument, was no ground of exception in a case not capital.

In *State* v. *Dry,* 152 N. C. 813 (1910), the charge being murder, one of the defendants, while the jury was being selected, had left the courtroom and gone into an adjoining room, for a short while, to speak with the coroner, without the knowledge of the court, solicitor or his counsel. The court withdrew a juror and ordered a mistrial, but refused to discharge the prisoner. This action was approved by the Supreme Court.

In *State* v. *Cherry,* 154 N. C. 624 (1911), the defendants had absented themselves from the courtroom on the morning the trial was to be continued. The court proceeded to finish the case and the defendants were found guilty and sentence imposed. Later defendants were apprehended and appealed to the Supreme Court where it was held to be an error to pass sentence upon them in their absence, so the case was remanded that a lawful sentence might be imposed.

In *State* v. *Wilcox,* 131 N. C. 707 (1902), defendant was on trial for murder. While defendant's counsel was addressing the jury, about one hundred people, being one-fourth of those in the courtroom, simultaneously, and as if by agreement, left the room. Soon thereafter a fire alarm was given near the courthouse, which caused a number of other people to leave. The trial judge, in his statement of the case, found that these demonstrations were for the purpose of breaking the force of the counsel's argument, but did not find that the jury was influenced thereby. On appeal it was held that, though there was no such finding, the disorderly proceedings were such as to warrant the Court in declaring that the trial was not conducted according to the law of the land, as guaranteed by the constitutional provision that no person ought to be deprived of life, liberty, or property but by the law of the land.

In *State* v. *Harrison,* 145 N. C. 408 (1907), defendant

was charged with kidnaping. On a sharp retort made by the state's counsel when the defense counsel interrupted his argument to correct a statement, a large part of the crowd in the courtroom applauded. The court rebuked the audience in strong terms and imprisoned one man for the disturbance. In his charge he told the jury that they' would be unworthy to sit in the jury box if they permitted the applause or any statement of the audience to sway them in the least from their duty. On appeal the Court found no error and stated that the defendant had no just cause of complaint.

In *State* v. *Nowell,* 156 N. C. 648 (1911), the defendant, a white woman, was charged with abduction. While argument of counsel for the defendant was in progress, and while denouncing the introduction of a negro to prove defendant's bad character, there was great applause, and the court had one woman arrested and seated on the prisoner's bench in full view of the jury. It was held that, in the absence of anything to show gross abuse of the lower court's discretion, its conduct was not reviewable.

In *State* v. *Ledford,* 133 N. C. 714 (1903), defendant was indicted for setting fire to and burning a barn. An appeal was taken on the ground that it did not appear in the record that the bill of indictment was returned in open court, but upon examination of the record the Court held that the exception was untenable because the court appeared to have been properly organized as required by law, according to the minutes.

In *State* v. *Bazemore,* 193 N. C. 336 (1927), defendant was charged with murder in the first degree and convicted. On appeal a new trial was awarded because the verdict was not received in open court in the presence of the presiding judge under Constitutional Mandate, Constitution, Article I, Sections 13, 17, which right may not be waived.

In a few cases there was an apparent denial of justice because of the employment of the wrong procedure or because the proper steps were not taken at the proper time. It cannot, in reality, be said that there was a denial of justice or that there would have been such denial if the case had been properly before the court. Regardless of the merits of the case or the wrongs suffered by the litigants, the courts are powerless to hear and act upon cases not properly before them. It is a well established rule in court procedure that a demurrer to the evidence in a criminal case must be taken before the verdict.[1] If the evidence is so weak and conflicting as to justify a demurrer, which is not taken, the defendant has no cause of complaint that his motion for demurrer is disallowed after the verdict. Under our statutes an objection to venue must be taken by a plea in abatement.[2] If the defendant relies upon a demurrer to the evidence to raise objection to venue and his motion is overruled and the case is decided against him, it seems that it is his counsel and not the court that is to blame if there is a substantial denial of justice. It has been uniformly held that one who fails, with full knowledge of the facts, to file his plea of abatement in apt time will be deemed to have waived his rights thereto.[3] A motion to nonsuit must of course be made at the proper time or it will be denied. It has been held that if a motion has been denied and further evidence is then introduced, the defendant loses the benefit of his first motion.[4] The action of the trial judge,

[1] *State* v. *Houston,* 155 N. C. 432 (1911) ; 156 N. C. 643 (1911).

[2] *Consolidated Statutes,* sec. 4606.

[3] *State* v. *Holder,* 133 N. C. 709 (1903) ; *State* v. *Lytle,* 117 N. C. 799 (1895) ; *State* v. *Woodard,* 183 N. C. 710 (1898).

[4] *State* v. *Killian,* 173 N. C. 792 (1911) ; *State* v. *Moore,* 120 N. C. 570 (1898).

in determining the qualifications of a juryman, if erroneous, is of course ground for challenging the array. The proper procedure is a motion to quash and set aside the entire panel. If the defendant fails to make such motion in apt time, he cannot be heard to complain after the trial and judgment. Technicalities of the type just indicated may have worked some injustice from the common sense, non-technical view point, but there is much in favor of the rules, and the remedy is a fuller conformity to them.

MISCONDUCT OF THE COURT

Table VI[5] shows that five cases were reversed by the Supreme Court on account of the misconduct of the trial judge. There were other instances where there was alleged misconduct on the part of the court but upon review the Supreme Court found no reversible error. We give below the main points in the cases reversed, because they describe the nature of the misconduct and the attitude of the Court.

In *State* v. *Swink,* 151 N. C. 726 (1909), on a trial for selling liquor, the trial judge committed the defendant's witness to custody for perjury while on the witness stand. This was held to be a reversible error, an invasion of the rights of the party who had offered the witness and an intimation of opinion prohibited by statute; therefore, a new trial was awarded.

In *State* v. *Cook,* 162 N. C. 586 (1913), there was an indictment for murder in which self-defense was being pleaded. There was evidence tending to show that the prisoner was unsuccessfully endeavoring to retreat from an attack made on him by the deceased and one P. with sticks, and that the third assailant, having made threats, had se-

[5] See *supra,* p. 33.

cured a gun and was returning with the gun, pointing it at the prisoner; it appears that while the attorney for the prisoner was arguing to the jury that because of the advance on the prisoner by the deceased and P., both with sticks, the latter known by the prisoner to be a man of violent character, the prisoner had a good and lawful reason for firing the fatal shot, the court interrupted him by saying, "what difference does it make if P. was advancing on him with a stick? That would not give him the right to kill the deceased." The Court held that the remark of the judge in the hearing of the jury, was an expression of his opinion on the evidence, which constitutes a reversible error, and it is not cured by an instruction that the jury are the sole judges of the evidence.

In *State* v. *Rogers,* 173 N. C. 755 (1912), the defendant was indicted for cruelty to animals. The Court held that a remark to the defendant by the trial judge, when testifying in his own behalf, to answer the questions asked him concisely, "and not to be dodging," is an expression of opinion on the credibility of the evidence, forbidden by statute, and constitutes a reversible error.

In *State* v. *Sparks,* 184 N. C. 745 (1922), defendant was on trial for violation of the prohibition laws. He had not admitted his guilt, but the trial judge in his charge to the jury, assumed that he was guilty upon the evidence of a state's witness. This was held to be an expression of opinion by the judge whether a fact has been fully or sufficiently proven and constitutes a reversible error.

In *State* v. *Bryant,* 189 N. C. 112 (1924), defendant was convicted of murder in the second degree. A new trial was awarded because the judge during the giving of the evidence on the trial, and in the presence of the jury remarked, "This witness has the weakest voice or the shortest memory of any witness I ever saw."

Misconduct of Counsel

Table VI[6] shows eight cases reversed because of misconduct of counsel during the trial. The results here are almost as gratifying as in the case of misconduct of the court itself. The following cases show the nature of the errors committed:

In *State* v. *Exum,* 138 N. C. 599 (1905), it was held by the Supreme Court that comments of counsel in argument to a jury are under the supervision of the trial judge, and the Court will not interfere with the exercise of his discretion unless it plainly appears that he has been too vigorous or too lax in the exercise of it, to the detriment of the parties.

In *State* v. *Tuten,* 131 N. C. 701 (1902), defendant was tried for selling liquor. The solicitor in addressing the jury said "This moonshine business must be broken up; Clayton's murder was caused by the moonshine business and you should put a stop to it." There was no evidence offered as to the murder of Clayton except in answer to a question on cross examination. The matter was not cured by any instruction of the judge, and the Court held that the improper remarks of the solicitor in the case constituted a ground for a new trial, because such statements were not in the evidence and were not properly admissible in the argument of counsel.

In *State* v. *Goode,* 132 N. C. 982 (1903), defendant was on trial for murder and it was held that where an attorney for the defendant comments upon the fact that the state had not subpoenaed certain persons having knowledge of the crime, it was error to allow the solicitor to state that the witnesses were subpoenaed by the defendant and were in court, there being no evidence of these facts, so a new trial was ordered.

In *State* v. *Tyson,* 133 N. C. 692 (1903), defendant, a

[6] See *supra,* p. 33.

former slave, was convicted of burning a tobacco barn. The only exception was to certain remarks of the solicitor "It did not appear that he (the defendant) was strongly attached to his old master and his family, as it appeared that when the test came he had a gun in his hand and ready to shoot down his young master, and is now drawing a pension for it." This case was affirmed on appeal by the court, but it turned on the fact that the exception was not taken in apt time. Montgomery and Douglas wrote lengthy dissenting opinions. No doubt defendant was prejudiced by the remark of the solicitor and was entitled to a new trial, but it is one of those cases where there was probably an injustice growing out of a legal technicality, which might have been avoided by more care and foresight on the part of counsel for the defense.

In *State* v. *Evans,* 183 N. C. 758 (1922), where the defendant was on trial for the manufacture of liquor, and the court had told the solicitor that it was improper for him to argue to the jury matters not in evidence, as that certain offenders carried spirituous liquors for a considerable distance into other states for the purpose of sale, the remarks of the solicitor thereafter that the jury all know that this was done, was held to be prejudicial to the defendant, entitling him to a new trial under the evidence of the case.

In *State* v. *Humphrey,* 186 N. C. 533 (1923), defendant was convicted of an assault on a female. In granting a new trial the Court held that the solicitor may not comment to the jury in a criminal action, on the failure of the defendant to testify at the trial in his own behalf, or the bad character of the defendant as a substantive fact to show guilt, when the defendant had not himself put his character in evidence on the issue.

In *State* v. *Tucker and Taylor,* 190 N. C. 708 (1925), defendants were charged with violating the prohibition laws and convicted. Defendants had not gone on the witness stand, but counsel for the state in his closing argument to the jury

commented upon the appearance of the defendants as follows, "Gentlemen of the jury, look at the defendants, they
look like professional bootleggers, their looks are enough
to convict them." This comment was not corrected by the
judge and was held to be a reversible error.

In *State* v. *Corpening,* 157 N. C. 621 (1911), defendant
was convicted of seduction. It was held to be a reversible
error for the solicitor to be permitted to read the facts
stated in an opinion of the Supreme Court related to a trial
for seduction and say, over objection of the defendant, that
the jury had convicted the defendant in that case under
weaker evidence than in the case at bar.

HABEAS CORPUS PROCEEDINGS

To Table VI might be added a group of twenty-
three *habeas corpus* cases in which a criminal offense
was charged and the procedure was by writ of *habeas
corpus.* But since *habeas corpus* is in the nature of a
writ employed to recover a person's liberty from illegal
restraint, it is well to consider these cases under a
separate heading. It is not necessary to set forth the
constitutional and statutory provisions regulating procedure in *habeas corpus* since we are concerned not so
much with the procedure as the result. Of the twenty-
three cases carried to the Supreme Court six were dismissed because the writ of *habeas corpus* did not lie
or because the Court refused to issue a writ of *certiorari* to bring the case up. With regard to the right of
the prisoner to appeal the Court said:

As this section guarantees the writ of habeas corpus, although there is no right of appeal given in such a case, the
Supreme Court, where it appears that a judge has refused
to hear evidence or to investigate the case on the return of
the writ, because it appears that a true bill has been found

against the prisoner by a grand jury, will exercise its constitutional power of supervision over the lower courts (Art. IV, Sec. 8) by writ of certiorari.[7]

In *State* v. *Hooker,* 183 N. C. 763 (1922), it was held that except in cases concerning the care and custody of children no appeal lies from a judgment in *habeas corpus* proceeding, but the action of the court may be reviewed, if at all, by writ of certiorari, which rests in the sound discretion of the appellate court.

With regard to the right of the state to appeal the Court said:

The State has no right of appeal in *habeas corpus* proceedings, as such proceedings must necessarily be summary to be useful, and if action could be arrested by an appeal upon the part of the State, the great writ of liberty would be deprived of its most beneficial results.[8]

Of the twelve cases affirmed, ten were refusals to discharge the prisoner from custody, while only two discharges were affirmed. This seems to indicate that discharge by writ of *habeas corpus* is not the usual thing; in fact, discharge appears to be quite the exception. Four cases were reversed, or reversed and remanded. The *Constitution,* Article I, Section 18, states very plainly that every person restrained of his liberty is entitled to a remedy to inquire into the lawfulness thereof, and to remove the same, if unlawful; and that such remedy ought not to be denied or delayed. But the courts have given both the Constitution and the statutes a strict interpretation which has at least limited the chances for abuse and discouraged the making of promiscuous applications for such writs.

[7] *State* v. *Herndon,* 107 N. C. 934 (1890).
[8] *In re Williams,* 149 N. C. 436 (1908).

In *re Schenck*, 74 N. C. 607 (1876), it was held that a writ of *habeas corpus* will not issue where the applicant is detained by virtue of a final judgment of a court of competent jurisdiction; and said writ will not issue when applicant is imprisoned in the State's Prison and the sentence of the court is erroneous. The applicant in default of appeal, must be left to his remedy by *certiorari*.

In *ex parte McCown*, 139 N. C. 95 (1905), it was held that a writ of *habeas corpus* can not be made to perform the functions of a writ of error. In the same case it was held that in order to warrant the discharge of a petitioner, the sentence under which he is held, must not only be erroneous, but absolutely void.

In *State* v. *Webb*, 155 N. C. 426 (1911), defendant was committed by a justice of the peace for a felony, and on the last day of the next subsequent term of court the action was continued on motion of the State for the absence of a material witness from sickness, whereupon the defendant, having given notice in open court, appeared and demanded that a bill of indictment be found at the next subsequent term, and that he be tried then, and that if an indictment were not then found he would pray for his discharge, which was done accordingly and the case further continued to the next term, owing to the continued sickness of the witness. On appeal it was held that there being no final judgment, an appeal would not lie from the refusal of the motion by the lower court, so the appeal was dismissed.

In the above case Mr. Justice Hoke pointed out that the existing statute might work an injustice to the petitioner, as it most surely did in this case. So in 1913 the Legislature made an amendment to the law. Under the old rule, the *Webb* case showed clearly that the defendant might be detained in prison for an indefinite time without a hearing, which of course is contrary to both the letter and spirit of the State Constitution. Under such conditions the prisoner was an unfortunate victim of circumstances and that not of his own fault. The Statute of 1913[9] is fully in accord with the Constitution and the spirit of right and justice.

[9] When any person who has been committed for treason or felony, plainly and specially expressed in the warrant of commitment, upon his prayer in open court to be brought to his trial, shall not be indicted some time in the next term of the superior or criminal court ensuing such commitment, the judge of the court upon notice in open court on the last day of the term, shall set at liberty such prisoner upon bail, unless it appears upon oath that the witness for the state could not be produced at the same term; and if such prisoner, upon his prayer as aforesaid, shall not be indicted and tried at the second term of the court, he shall be discharged from his imprisonment: Provided, the judge presiding may, in his discretion, refuse to discharge such prisoner if the time between the first and the second terms of the court be less than four months. *Public Laws,* 1913, c. 2.

CHAPTER XI

LEGISLATION GOVERNING CRIMINAL PROCEDURE

THE STATE Constitution of 1868 provides that in all criminal prosecutions every man has the right to be informed of the accusation against him, to confront the accusers and witnesses with other testimony, to have counsel for his defense, and not to be compelled to give evidence against himself. He shall not be put to answer any criminal charge (except as otherwise provided) but by indictment, presentment, or impeachment. He shall not be convicted of any crime but by the unanimous verdict of a jury of good and lawful men in open court. Excessive bail shall not be required, nor excessive fines imposed, nor cruel or unusual punishment inflicted. When restrained of his liberty he is entitled to a remedy to enquire into the lawfulness thereof and such remedy ought not to be delayed or denied. All courts shall be open and every person for injury done him, etc., shall have remedy by due course of law, and rights and justice administered without sale, denial or delay (see *supra* p. 36).

At the time of the adoption of the Constitution a great many laws were in force governing criminal procedure which in no way conflicted with the Constitution and so were continued in force. Among these were general provisions concerning the statute of limitations for misdemeanors, recognizances, venue, presentments, indictments, challenges and appeals. The Legislature which met immediately following the adoption of the Constitution 1868-69 pretty thoroughly reorganized court procedure along lines consistent with the new

Constitution. In some instances new statutes were needed to supplement the work of the constitutional convention, and in other cases experience had taught the legislators that old methods of procedure were inadequate and must give way to simpler and more effective forms. We are indebted to the Session of 1868-69 for the bulk of the procedural laws under which we now operate. At this session laws were passed regarding speedy trials, the issuance of warrants, peace warrants, arrests, fugitives from justice, preliminary examinations, bail, forfeiture of bail, commitment to prison, trials before justices of the peace, and appeals. Various statutes have been modified and new ones added from time to time to meet new needs and particular difficulties.

It is not directly within the scope of this study to consider procedural statutes except in so far as they have affected the cases which have been carried to the Supreme Court. But a number of statutes which apply strictly to procedure in the Superior Courts have had at least an indirect influence upon the work of the Supreme Court, and we shall give some space to them. Certain other statutes have done much to facilitate the administration of justice while others have had a tendency to delay and block its course. These, of course, should be mentioned. It is necessary to go back of the period of this study (1890) for an understanding of the course of legislation because many of the most important laws were passed before this time.

STATUTES GOVERNING APPEALS

Under the common law the defendant had no right of appeal and was forced to sue out a writ of error if he sought to have a decision of the lower court reviewed. However, in this State the right of review is fixed by statute. In 1875 the writ of error was abolished in civil actions and in 1911 this rule was applied to criminal actions.[1] The right of appeal is secured by statute and the courts have been careful to see that all the requirements are fully complied with.

The State Constitution, Article IV, Section 8, provides that:

The Supreme Court shall have jurisdiction to review, upon appeal, any decision of the Courts below, upon any matter of law or legal inference. And the jurisdiction of said Court over "issues of fact" and "questions of facts" shall be the same exercised by it before the adoption of the Constitution of one thousand eight hundred and sixty-eight, and the Courts shall have the power to issue any remedial writs necessary to give it general supervision and control over the proceedings of the Inferior Courts.

As early as 1818 the Legislature passed the following important statute with regard to appeals defining the rights of the appellant, etc. It is now Section 638 of the *Consolidated Statutes,* and is as follows:

An appeal may be taken from any judicial order or determination of any judge of the superior court, upon or involving a matter of law or legal inference, whether made in or out of term, which affects a substantial right claimed in any action, and permits a judgment from which an appeal might be taken, or discontinues the action, or grants or refuses a new trial.

It appears from the language of the statute that the right of appeal is broad and general. But this right has

[1] *State* v. *Webb,* 155 N. C. 426 (1911).

been limited to some extent by other statutes. For example in the same year a law was passed with regard to the giving of security and is now Section 4650 of the *Consolidated Statutes:*

In all cases of conviction in the superior court of any criminal offense, the defendant shall have the right of appeal, on giving adequate security to abide the sentence, judgment or decree of the supreme court; and the appeal shall be perfected and the case for the supreme court settled, as provided in civil actions.

In 1870 the Legislature passed an act providing that convicted persons may appeal without giving security for costs. It is now Section 4651 of the *Consolidated Statutes,* and is as follows:

In all such cases of conviction in the said courts the defendant shall have the right of appeal without giving costs, upon filing an affidavit that he is wholly unable to give security for costs, and is advised by counsel that he has reasonable cause for the appeal prayed, and that the application is in good faith.

There is no doubt that one of the great safeguards against injustice and possible judicial prejudice is the right of appeal. The entire system of courts should be open at all times to the poor as well as the rich. In view of the large number of reversals there can be no doubt that the statute permitting appeals in *forma pauperis* has served a good purpose. An examination of the records of the cases showed that a great many appeals have been taken under this statute. The pauper statute when considered alone would indicate that it might be easily abused; for instance, the defendant must file an affidavit that he is "wholly unable to give security for costs, and is advised by counsel that he has reasonable cause for the appeal prayed, and that the application is in good faith." If the mere taking of the oath were the only requirement, the statute would no doubt be more abused than it is now. But the case on appeal is made out by the judge and, if the defendant is fraudulently using the pauper statute, the solicitor, of course, can make inquiry into the financial status of the applicant. The statute seems to assume that the solicitor will always be on guard to prevent any abuses or irregularities in this matter. We can not say that this statute is abused but it is much used. It would not work a hardship on the pauper defendant to require further evidence of his inability to meet the appeal bond than his oath, and it certainly would not prevent the employment of the full benefit of the statute in worthy cases. On the other hand, it might prevent some pauper appeals when the defendant is able to meet the bond but appeals to delay the execution of the judgment because he can do so without cost.

Consolidated Statutes, Section 1421, provides that "the justices of the supreme court shall prescribe and establish from time to time rules of practice for that court and also for the superior courts. . . ."

In *State* v. *Ward,* 184 N. C. 618 (1922), the Court said, "The rules prescribed by the Supreme Court to regulate its own procedure, including the rule as to dismissing an appeal thereto if not docketed, or a recordari prayed for in apt time, will be strictly enforced, being under the exclusive authority therein given to the Supreme Court Article I, Section 8 of the Constitution."

With regard to the time of taking an appeal a statute was passed in 1889 and is now Section 641 of the *Consolidated Statutes:*

The appeal must be taken from a judgment rendered out of term within ten days after notice thereof, and from a judgment rendered in term within ten days after the rendition, unless the record shows an appeal taken at the trial, which is sufficient, but execution shall not be suspended until the giving by the appellant of the undertaking hereinafter required.

One of the chief criticisms of criminal procedure in some jurisdictions is delay between the time the crime is committed and the final disposition of the case. The State Constitution places the delay of justice in the same category with its denial, and the Legislature seemed to have been keenly awake to the spirit of the Constitution in the passage of the law as to the time for taking appeals. It will be noted that ten days is allotted unless the appeal is taken at the trial. The time for serving notice on the opposite party is fifteen days, and the party so served has ten days in which to respond.[2] But Section 664 of the *Consolidated Statutes*, requires that the judge shall settle the case on appeal within sixty days after the courts of the district have ended or be subject to a fine of $500. Under the normal course of procedure the case will come before the Supreme Court at the next regular term, and be disposed of. It is a rule of the Supreme Court that in making up the docket from each district the criminal cases are placed at the head of the list and are first disposed of. Any appeal may, of course, be abandoned by the defendant, but this would mean the forfeiture of the appeal bond and the immediate execution of the judgment. Any process as complex as the taking of an appeal takes time and involves some delay. There

[2] *Consolidated Statutes,* sec. 643.

are certain matters left to the discretion of the trial judge which may cause some delay, but on the whole it seems that the laws are such that they do not readily lend themselves to purely dilatory tactics.

In planning this study we had hoped to treat this matter rather fully in this State but further investigation has shown the impossibility of doing so with regard to the cases appealed to the Supreme Court. Unfortunately, at least for the purpose of research, the *Supreme Court Reports* have been annotated and abbreviated from time to time until certain valuable facts have entirely disappeared. Except in *per curiam* cases the date of the trial in the Superior Court is usually given. The date when the offense was committed may or may not appear in the Supreme Court's report of the case, depending on whether the bill of indictment is set forth in full or not, and whether the date was brought out in the testimony which the Court is considering in deciding the case. If this information were readily available, we would still have the task of taking each case separately and going to the original docket of the Supreme Court to see on what day the decision was rendered, because only the term and not the day of the decision is given in the reports. The task would be still further complicated by trying to follow up those cases in which a new trial was awarded, etc. We are wholly without information as to delays in the Superior Courts. With regard to the time elapsing between the trial in the lower court and final disposition by the Supreme Court our opinion is somewhat conjectural. But taking into consideration all the statutes on appeal and the rules of the court in connection with the cases we conclude that by and large, most cases are disposed of in a reasonable length of time upon appeal to the Supreme Court.

STATUTES GOVERNING INDICTMENTS

Another important group of statutes has had to do with the matter of indictments. From time to time the Legislature has passed laws simplifying and making certain forms of indictment sufficient. Many of the technical absurdities so characteristic of indictments during the early period were removed by express statutory enactment before 1890, and for that reason there have been fewer significant changes both in the laws and rulings of the court since that time than one would expect. We have noted under the heading of "Defective Indictments" (see *supra* p. 48, *et seq.*), something of the constructive work of the courts in the simplification of indictments. Without going into the cases and procedural difficulties which have resulted in statutory changes, we shall briefly consider some of the laws.

In 1842 a law with regard to indictments for subornation of perjury was passed which is as follows:

In every indictment for subornation of perjury, or for corrupt bargaining or contracting with others to commit wilful and corrupt perjury, it is sufficient to set forth the substance of the offense charged upon the defendant, without setting forth the bill, answer, information, indictment, declaration or any part of any record or proceedings, and without setting forth the commission or authority of the court or person before whom the perjury was committed or was agreed or promised to be committed.[3]

[3] *Revisal,* s. 3248 (1842), c. 49, sec. 2; *Consolidated Statutes,* 4616.

In 1852 the Legislature passed the following statute relative to indictments with intent to defraud and to larceny and receiving.

In any case where an intent to defraud is required to constitute the offense of forgery, or any other offense whatever, it is sufficient to allege in the indictment an intent to defraud, without naming therein the particular person or body corporate intended to be defrauded; and on the trial of such indictment, it shall be sufficient, and shall not be deemed a variance, if there appear to be an intent to defraud the United States, or any state, county, city, town or parish, or body corporate, or any public officer, in his official capacity, or any copartnership or member thereof, or any particular person. The defendant may be charged in the same indictment in several counts with separate offenses or receiving stolen goods, knowing them to be stolen, and larceny.[4]

In the manner of alleging joint ownership of property the following statute was passed:

In any indictment wherein it is necessary to state the ownership of any property whatsoever, whether real or personal, which belongs to or is in possession of, more than one person, whether such persons be partners in trade, joint tenants or tenants in common, it is sufficient to name one of such persons, and to state such property to belong to the person so named, and another or others, as the case may be; and whenever, in any such indictment, it is necessary to mention, for any purpose whatever, any partners, joint tenants or tenants in common, it is sufficient to describe them in the manner aforesaid; and this provision shall extend to all joint stock companies and trustees.[5]

[4] *Revisal*, s. 3253 (1852), c. 87, sec. 2; *Consolidated Statutes*, 4621.

[5] *Revisal*, s. 3250; *Consolidated Statutes*, 4618.

In 1873 a law was passed declaring that certain defects in indictments do not vitiate.

No judgment upon any indictment for felony or misdemeanor, whether after verdict, or by confession or otherwise, shall be stayed or reversed for the want of the averment of any matter unnecessary to be proved, nor for omission of the words "as appears of record," or of the words "with force and arms," nor for the insertion of the words "against the form of the statutes," instead of the words "against the form of the statute," or *vice versa;* nor for omitting to state the time at which the offense was committed, in any case where time is not of the essence of the offense, nor for stating the time imperfectly, nor for stating the offense to have been committed on a day subsequent to the finding of the indictment, or on an impossible day, or on a day that never happened; nor for want of a proper and perfect venue, when the court shall appear by the indictment to have had jurisdiction of the offense.[6]

In 1871-72 a law was passed simplifying indictments for embezzlement as follows:

In indictments for embezzlement, except when the offense relates to a chattel, it is sufficient to allege the embezzlement to be of money, without specifying any particular coin or valuable security; and such allegation, so far as regards the description of the property, shall be sustained if the offender shall be proved to have embezzled any amount, although the particular species of coin or valuable security of which such amount was composed shall not be proved.[7]

In general keeping with the above law concerning embezzlement the Legislature of 1876-77 modified indictments concerning larceny of money as follows:

[6] *Revisal,* c. 35, S20 (1873) ; *Consolidated Statutes,* 4625.

[7] *Revisal,* s. 3252 (1871-72), c. 145, sec. 2; *Consolidated Statutes,* 4620.

In every indictment in which it is necessary to make any averment as to the larceny of any money, or United States treasury note, or any note of any bank whatsoever, it is sufficient to describe such money, or treasury note, or bank note, simply as money, without specifying any particular coin, or treasury note, or bank note; and such allegation so far as regards the description of property, shall be sustained by proof of any amount of coin, or treasury note, or bank note, although the particular species of coin, of which such amount was composed, or the particular nature of the treasury note, or bank note, shall be proven.[8]

Finally in 1887 the Legislature passed a law simplifying indictments for murder and manslaughter as follows:

That in bills of indictment for murder and manslaughter, it shall not be necessary to allege a matter not required to be proved on the trial; but in the body of the indictment, after naming the person or persons accused, and the county of his or their residence, the date of the offense, the averment "with force of arms," and the county of the alleged commission of the offense, as is now usual, it shall be sufficient in describing murder to allege that the accused person or persons (as the case may be), feloniously, wilfully, and of his or their malice aforethought, did kill and murder (naming the person killed), and concluding as aforesaid; and any bill of indictment containing the averments and allegations herein named shall be good and sufficient in law as an indictment for murder or manslaughter as the case may be.[9]

In 1889 the following law was passed regulating indictments for perjury:

[8] *Revisal*, s. 3251 (1876-77), c. 68; *Consolidated Statutes*, 4619.

[9] *Consolidated Statutes*, 4614.

In any indictment for wilful and corrupt perjury it is sufficient to set forth the substance of the offense charged upon the defendant and by what court, or before whom, the oath was taken (avering such court or person to have competent authority to administer the same), together with the proper averments to falsify the matter wherein the perjury is assigned, without setting forth the bill, answer, information, indictment, declaration, or any part of any record or proceedings, either in law or equity, other than aforesaid, and without setting forth the commission or authority of the court or person before whom the perjury was committed.[10]

The progressive trend of the Legislature is quite apparent in this group of laws governing indictments. Everywhere the tendency has been toward simplification and elimination of superfluities and nonessentials. One of the great constructive safeguards to a person accused of crime is the right to be informed of the accusation against him, and his right should be diligently and zealously preserved at all times; but a criminal should not be permitted to escape justice purely on the ground of some legal technicality when legislative intent, evidence, and common sense are all to the contrary, and when no real violence will occur either to the spirit or letter of the law by sustaining an indictment. The work of the Legislature and the courts before 1890 was indeed commendable. There was an occasional lapse into making fine and critical distinctions and sometimes an over devotion to the principle of *stare decisis,* but the period is marked by progress, and a decision like *State* v. *Carter* would have been impossible in 1890.

[10] *Revisal,* s. 3246-47; *Code,* 1185 (1889), c. 83; *Consolidated Statutes,* 4615.

THE POWER TO AMEND WARRANTS

Another important group of statutes has to do with the process of amending warrants. The statutes with regard to this matter are liberal and the right of amendment has no doubt prevented many guilty persons from escaping punishment upon the pretext of some technical defect in the warrant. Not only has the Legislature been liberal in the passage of laws, but also the courts have given them a broad and progressive interpretation for which they deserve much credit. As early as 1794 a statute was passed which, with amendments, is now Section 1500 of the *Consolidated Statutes,* Rule 12, which is as follows:

No process or other proceedings begun before a justice of the peace, whether in a civil or criminal action, shall be quashed or set aside, for want of form, if essential matters are set forth therein; and the court in which any such action shall be pending shall have power to amend any warrant, process, pleading or proceeding in such action, either in form or substance, for furtherance of justice, on such terms as shall be deemed just, either before or after judgment.

In *State* v. *Mills,* 181 N. C. 530 (1921), in commenting on the above statute the Court said:

The reason for the change in the statute extending the power of amendment, so as to include both civil and criminal cases, matters of substance as well as matters of form, and power to amend before or after judgment, is perfectly obvious. It was because a justice of the peace was supposed to lack the technical learning in framing the process and pleadings, whereas the lawyer who practiced in the Superior Courts, and the solicitor, were supposed to have both, and also the judge, and no harm could be done to the defendant, or to the opposite party, by making the process or pleading conform, in some degree, to the rules of law. It produced, at least greater certainty in legal procedure. No party could be prejudiced by it unless there was a departure from the original charge in the warrant.

On appeal from a court of a justice of the peace, the Superior Court judge may, under the section, Rule 12, liberally allow amendments in his discretion, to the substance of a criminal complaint, as well as to the form, when so doing does not change the character of the offense originally charged.

In 1831 a statute was passed which, with amendments, is now Section 1414 of the *Consolidated Statutes,* and is given in full below:

The supreme court has power to amend any process pleading or proceeding either in form or substance for the purpose of furthering justice, on such terms as shall be deemed just at any time before final judgment; and to amend by making proper parties to any case when the court may deem it necessary and proper for the purpose of justice and on such terms as the court may prescribe. And whenever it appears necessary for the purpose of justice, the court may allow and direct the taking of further testimony in any case which may be pending in the court, under such rules as may be prescribed, or may remand the case to the intent that amendments may be made, further testimony taken or other proceedings had in the court below.

In *State* v. *Poythress,* 174 N. C. 809 (1917), defendant was convicted of violating the prohibition laws. On appeal, for insufficient warrant, the court found no error and said "the policy of the law is to allow liberal amendments to the warrant of arrest, with the limitation that the amendment allowed must conform to the evidence elicited on the trial; and, in this case, on appeal from a recorder's court, and on trial in the Superior Court, under indictment for violating the state prohibition laws, the court properly allowed amendments alleging two additional counts, there being abundant evidence to sustain them."[11]

CHALLENGES TO THE JURY

One of the weak points in the jury system which has given the defendant a decided advantage over the state is the excessively large number of peremptory jury challenges given him in capital felonies. The *Revised Statutes of 1837* show that in the trial of capital cases the defendant was given thirty-five peremptory challenges of the jury.[12] But this statute was so amended that under the *Revisal of 1905* the number was reduced from thirty-five to twenty-three.[13] Again in 1913 the number was still further reduced to twelve. The present law is as follows:

Every person on joint or several trial for his life may make a peremptory challenge of twelve jurors and no more; and in all joint or several trials, for crimes and misdemeanors, other than capital, every person shall have the right of challenging peremptorily and without showing cause, four jurors and no more. And to enable defendant to exercise this right, the clerk in all such trials shall read over the names of the jurors on the panel, in the presence

---

[11] On the power of the courts to amend warrants see the following cases: *State* v. *Baker,* 106 N. C. 758 (1890); *State* v. *Yellowday,* 152 N. C. 793 (1910); *State* v. *Gillikin,* 114 N. C. 832 (1894); *State* v. *Price,* 175 N. C. 804 (1918); *State* v. *Telfair,* 130 N. C. 645 (1902); *State* v. *Hyman,* 164 N. C. 411 (1913); *State* v. *Publishing Co.,* 179 N. C. 720 (1920); *State* v. *Lee,* 164 N. C. 533 (1913).

[12] *Revised Statutes,* c. 35, sec. 21.

[13] *Revisal of 1905,* Raleigh, 1905, sec. 3263.

and hearing of the counsel before the jury shall be empaneled to try the issue; and the judge or other presiding officer of the court shall decide all questions as to the competency of the jurors.[14]

The right of the state to peremptory challenges is set forth in the following statute which was passed in 1827 and has been amended from time to time. The origin of this statute is 33 Edward I, c. 4.

In all capital cases the prosecuting officer on behalf of the State shall have the right to challenge peremptorily four jurors for each defendant, but shall not have the right to stand any jurors at the foot of the panel. The challenge must be made before the juror is tendered to the prisoner, and if he will challenge more than four jurors he shall assign for his challenge a cause certain; and in all other cases of a criminal nature, a challenge of two jurors shall be allowed in behalf of the state for each defendant and the same shall be inquired of according to the custom of the court.[15]

A mere glance at the two statutes shows clearly that all the points are in favor of the accused. While he cannot choose a jury, he has great power of rejection which if abused might result in a miscarriage of justice. It is difficult to see the logic of the two statutes. Perhaps the explanation is to be found in the rigors of early penalties when a minor offense was punishable by life imprisonment or death. Every safeguard was thrown about the man accused of crime, and his chances of acquittal far exceeded those of conviction. But cruel and unusual punishments are forbidden by the constitution, and there seems to be no good reason

[14] *Consolidated Statutes,* 4633.
[15] *Ibid.,* 4634.

for the defendant in a case having more peremptory challenges than the state. Twelve peremptory challenges by the defendant to four by the state is a legal absurdity carried over from the early days and has little or no justification. Of course it is argued that the defendant's right of challenging twelve jurors peremptorily is in favor of human life, and this is probably true; but it is also true that it increases the chances of acquittal, regardless of the guilt or innocence of the defendant. This is particularly true where a unanimous verdict of twelve jurors is required to convict. It seems that six peremptory challenges, both by the state and by the defendant would be fair and productive of better results.

With regard to peremptory challenges in non-capital offenses it seems that two peremptory challenges both by the state and by the defendant would be sufficient. If a man is really disqualified for jury service, he will more than likely be forced to retire under one of the various challenges for cause. If he is not disqualified for cause, the chances are that he will be an honest juror, though possibly not satisfactory to the defendant particularly if the latter is guilty.

STATUTE OF LIMITATIONS

In this state the statute of limitations for misdemeanors is prescribed by a special statute which provides that the prosecution must be brought within two years. There are, however, certain important exceptions to this rule. The law is contained in the *Consolidated Statutes,* Section 4512, and is as follows:

All misdemeanors and petit larceny where the value of the property does not exceed five dollars, except the offenses of perjury, forgery, malicious mischief, and other malicious misdemeanors, deceit, and the offense of being accessory after the fact, now made a misdemeanor, shall be presented or found by the grand jury within two years after the commission of the same, and not afterwards: Provided, that in case any of the misdemeanors, hereby required to be prosecuted within two years, shall have been committed in a secret manner, the same may be prosecuted within two years after the discovery of the offender: Provided further, that if any indictment found within that time shall be defective, so that no judgment can be given thereon, another prosecution may be instituted for the same offense, one year after the first shall have been abandoned by the state.

With regard to offenses of felony grade there is no specific statute, but the common-law rule of no limitation applies. In *State* v. *Mallet,* 125 N. C. 723 (1899), Justice Clark speaking for the court on this point said:

Up to the Act of 1891, Chapter 205, in this state, we followed the somewhat arbitrary common-law rule as to what crimes were felonies, and what were misdemeanors, and under that conspiracy, and even such grave crimes as perjury and forgery, were misdemeanors; by the Act of 1891, North Carolina adopted the rule, now almost universally prevalent, by which the nature of the punishment determines the classification of the offense, those which may be punished capitally or by imprisonment in the penitentiary are felonies (as to which there is no statute of limitations), and all others are misdemeanors, as to which prosecutions in this State are barred by two years.

WITNESS NOT EXCLUDED BY INTEREST OR CRIME

Under the common-law rule the testimony of a witness was carefully excluded in a criminal proceeding if it could be shown that he had an interest in the crime or matter at issue. Such a rule was manifestly unjust and often operated to the great disadvantage of the person accused of crime. The common-law rule was changed in this state by a series of statutes and amendments all of which are embodied in Section 1792 of the *Consolidated Statutes.* The law is as follows:

No person offered as a witness shall be excluded by reason of incapacity from interest or crime, from giving evidence either in person or by deposition, according to the practice of the court on the trial of any issue joined, or of any matter or question, or any inquiry arising in any suit or proceeding, civil or criminal . . . and every person so offered shall be admitted to give evidence, notwithstanding such person may or shall have an interest in the matter in question.

The introduction to the statute seems to express very well the difficulties out of which the statute grew and the attitude of the General Assembly on the matter:

Whereas, the inquiry for the truth in the courts of justice is often obstructed by incapacities created by the present law, and it is desirable that full information as to the facts in issue, both in criminal and civil cases, should be had before the persons appointed to decide upon them, and that such persons should exercise their judgments on the credit of the witness adduced, and on the truth of the testimony; now therefore, etc., etc.

New Trial and Demurrer to Evidence

Under the law of 1815, c. 459, which is now Section 4644 of the *Consolidated Statutes,* it is provided that the courts may grant new trials in criminal cases when the defendant is found guilty under the same rules and regulations as in civil cases. In 1897, 1899, and 1901, statutes were passed governing civil procedure and are now Section 567 of the *Consolidated Statutes*. But in the case of *State* v. *Hegan,* 131 N. C. 803 (1902), these statutes were held not to apply to criminal actions. In 1913 the following statute was passed which in effect overruled the Hegan case and shortened and simplified the procedure with regard to motions for nonsuit. It is now Section 4643 of the *Consolidated Statutes*.

When on the trial of any criminal action in the superior court, or any criminal court, the state has produced its evidence and rested its case, the defendant may move to dismiss the action or for a judgment of nonsuit. If the motion is allowed, judgment shall be entered accordingly; and such judgment shall have the force and effect of a verdict of "not guilty" as to such defendant. If the motion is refused, the defendant may except; and if the defendant introduces no evidence, the case shall be submitted to the jury as in other cases, and the defendant shall have the benefit of his exception on appeal to the supreme court.

Nothing in this section shall prevent the defendant from introducing evidence after his motion for nonsuit has been overruled; and he may again move for a judgment of nonsuit after the evidence in the case is concluded. If the motion is then refused, upon consideration of all the evidence, the defendant may except; and after the jury has rendered its verdict, he shall have the benefit of such latter exception on appeal to the supreme court. If the defendant's motion for judgment of nonsuit be granted, or be sustained on appeal to the supreme court, it shall in all cases have the force and effect of a verdict of "not guilty."

COURT STENOGRAPHERS

Sometimes judges complain that they were reversed on appeal because they were incorrectly quoted in their charge to the jury. It seems this complaint is more common in the case of older judges or ex-judges. There are, no doubt, isolated cases of this sort but they are exceptional and occur less frequently each year. A number of counties in the state have regular court stenographers whose business it is to take down the proceedings of the court. These stenographers range no doubt in ability from very good to very poor. Regardless of their responsibility, their willingness to serve, and their oath, some of them are inefficient and inaccuracies will creep in.

In 1913, an act was passed by the Legislature which provided that upon the request of any judge holding a Superior Court in any county in the state, the board of county commissioners shall employ a competent stenographer to take down the proceedings of the court.

Every stenographer is to make three copies of the proceedings in every case appealed to the Supreme Court, without extra charge, and furnish one copy to the attorneys on each side, and file one copy with the clerk of the Superior Court of the county in which any such case is tried, and shall obey all orders of the judge relative to the time in which such work shall be done.

Every such stenographer so employed shall before entering upon the discharge of his duties, be duly sworn to well, truly, and correctly take down and transcribe the proceedings of the court, except the argument of the counsel, and the charge of the court thus taken down and transcribed shall be held to be a compliance with the law requiring the judge to put his instruction to the jury in writing.[16]

[16] "This section shall not apply to any county which has a court stenographer authorized by law. . . . This act shall not

It is not possible to find out how widely this law is applied without going into great detail. It will be noted that the matter is discretionary with the trial judge, and he may or may not ask for a stenographer.

ADDRESSES OF ATTORNEYS TO THE JURY

Criticism has been occasioned in the past by the addresses of counsel to the jury. We have a feeling that much of the criticism has been just and that the taxpayer has been perfectly justified in protesting against being forced to finance Marathon eloquence. The old style of courtroom oratory, boisterous, biting, or sentimental is rapidly disappearing, but the final word has not yet been spoken in the matter. Our present system is not satisfactory and there will doubtless be further changes in the near future. Statutes have been passed from time to time governing these addresses. Early practice assumed that the judge had full control over the addresses, and if the attorney was permitted to appear before the jury it was by courtesy of the judge presiding. By 1837, there was a law that not more than one attorney could speak in any cause. By 1855, it had been so changed that not more than one attorney could speak unless allowed by the court. In 1874-75 the so-called Spears Act was passed which we quote in full:

Any attorney appearing in any civil or criminal action shall be entitled to address the court or the jury for such a space of time as in his opinion may be necessary for the

apply to the following counties: Alleghany, Brunswick, Caldwell, Camden, Carteret, Caswell, Chatham, Currituck, Dare, Davidson, Davie, Forsyth, Greene, Haywood, Hoke, New Hanover, Orange, Pender, Perquimans, Person, Surry, Transylvania, Union, Watauga." *Ex. Sess. 1913*, c. 69; *Consolidated Statutes*, 1461.

proper development and presentation of his case; and in jury trials he may argue to the jury the whole case as well of law as of fact.[17]

This law, on the very face of it, was of course unsatisfactory. In 1903 another law was passed regulating addresses. It is now Section 203 of the *Consolidated Statutes* and is as follows:

In all trials in the superior courts there shall be allowed two addresses to the jury for the state and two for the defendant, except in capital felonies where there shall be no limit as to the number. The judges of the superior court are also authorized to limit the time of argument on the trial of all actions, civil and criminal, except in capital felonies, but in no instance shall the time be limited to less than one hour on each side in misdemeanors, or to less than three hours on each side in other causes. When any greater number of addresses or extension of time shall be desired, motion shall be made, and it shall be in the discretion of the judge to allow the same or not, as the interests of justice may require. In jury trials the whole case as well of law as of fact may be argued to the jury (1903, c. 433).

The Legislature of 1927 amended the act to read as follows:

The judges of the Superior Court are authorized to limit the argument of counsel to the jury on trial of actions, civil and criminal as follows; to not less than one hour on each side in misdemeanors and appeals from Justices of the Peace; to not less than two hours on each side in all other civil actions and in felonies less than capital; in capital felonies, the time argument of Counsel may not be limited otherwise, than by consent, except that the Court may limit the number of those who may address the jury to three counsels on each side.

[17] (1874-75), c. 114.

In consideration of the fact that the trial judges know the law and the facts of each particular case, it seems that a statute might very well be passed investing them with the power of fixing the time limit each side shall have at its disposal in addressing the jury. The grade of the offense charged is no test of the length of time required to present it fairly and fully to the jury. An involved civil case may require a great deal more explanation than a clear-cut murder case. It is impossible for any group of legislators to pass a time limit statute that can be uniformly and satisfactorily applied to every case. Investing the judge with this power would be no departure from our established ideas, for there would be no greater exercise of discretionary powers in this case than the judge is called upon to exercise every day with regard to other matters.

CHAPTER XII

SUMMARY AND THE POSSIBILITIES OF JUDICIAL REFORM

THE JUDICIAL Department of the state of North Carolina consists of the Supreme Court, Superior Courts, Courts of Justices of the Peace, Recorder's Court and County Courts. There are twenty judicial districts in North Carolina with a judge and solicitor in each, elected by the voters of the district. By the system of rotation of judges, a trial judge holds court in the same district not oftener than once in four years except in cases of emergency.

During the period of this study (1890-1927 inclusive) 2,183 criminal cases were carried to the Supreme Court by appeal or by writ of certiorari. Of this number 341 cases, or 15.6 per cent, were dismissed because the defendant had failed to perfect his appeal or because the statutes and rules governing appeals had not been complied with.

The statute of 1883 gave the state a limited right of appeal on points of law only; namely, upon a special verdict, upon a demurrer, upon a motion to quash, and upon arrest of judgment.

ANALYSIS OF CASES DECIDED BY THE SUPREME COURT

Of the 1,842 criminal cases decided by the Supreme Court, 115 were *per curiam,* and so the appellant could not be determined by reading the cases in the *Supreme Court Reports.* Of the 1,544 cases in which the defendant appealed 1,054 were affirmed, 381 reversed and remanded, and 109 reversed. The state appealed in 183 cases. Of this number eighty-eight were affirmed, eighty-six reversed and remanded, and nine reversed. Of the total appeals 83 per cent were taken by the defendant, and 10 per cent by the state. The affirmances on appeal by the defendant were 68 per cent and on appeal by the state 47 per cent. On appeal by the defendant 24 per cent were reversed and remanded while on the state's appeal 46 per cent were reversed and remanded. The reversals on appeal by the defendant were 7 per cent, and on appeal by the state 5 per cent.

Of the 1,842 cases actually decided by the Supreme Court 1,243 were affirmed, 480 reversed and remanded, and 119 reversed—the percentages being 67.5, 26 and 6.5 respectively. Distributed over the whole period of the study the average number of cases dismissed per year was nine. The average number of cases decided by the Court each year was forty-eight. Of this number thirty-three were affirmed, twelve reversed and remanded, and three reversed.

It is necessary to consider the cases decided by the Supreme Court in comparison with the total number of cases disposed of in the Superior Courts in order to understand more fully the work of the two Courts. The *Biennial Reports of the Attorney General of North Carolina* indicate that during the period of this study (1890-1927 inclusive) 68 per cent of all criminal trials in the Superior Courts have resulted in convictions.[1]

[1] There may be a slight inaccuracy in these figures as the first *Report* was based on an eighteen-month period, only six months of which was within the period of this study. An average was made by dividing the total cases for eighteen months by three. As the Attorney General has not yet prepared his report for the last half of 1927, the first half was doubled for the purpose of this study.

A classification of the cases according to the nature of the offense committed shows 179 cases of murder in the first degree, 102 of murder in the second degree, 101 of manslaughter, ten of arson, ten of burglary in the first degree, eight of burglary in the second, twenty-eight of rape, seven of carnal knowledge, twenty-four of embezzlement, sixteen of forgery, thirty-three of false pretense, twenty-three of perjury, ninety-two of larceny, fourteen of highway robbery or larceny from the person, eighty-four of assault with deadly weapons, twenty-six of assault to rape, thirty-four of burning and 1,051 miscellaneous.

Errors Committed by the Lower Courts

The following were the more usual types of errors committed by the lower courts:

1. *Violation of Constitutional Provisions.* Twenty-two cases were reversed because some section of the state or federal Constitution had been violated. The sections most often before the courts have had to do with juries, former conviction or acquittal as a bar to further prosecution, self-incriminating testimony, presence of the defendant in the courtroom, and cruel or unusual punishment.

2. *Defective Indictments.* Forty-one cases were reversed because of defective bills of indictment. Technicalities and absurdities have been most apparent in the matter of indictments, but both by statute and by judicial interpretation indictments have been greatly simplified. All that is now required is for the offense to be sufficiently charged in the bill of indictment to enable the court to proceed to judgment.

3. *Quashed Cases.* There were forty reversals on account of quashed bills of indictment or arrests of judgment in the lower courts. The right of the state to appeal has

been effective in bringing these cases before the Supreme Court, whereas, without this right the cases would have ended in the lower courts.

4. *Variance between the Allegation and the Proof.* Eight cases were reversed because there was held to be a fatal variance between the allegation and the proof.

5. *Instruction to the Jury.* 231 cases were reversed because of improper instruction to the jury. More cases were reversed for this cause than for any other single reason. The law of 1796 prohibits the trial judge from giving an opinion as to whether a fact is fully or sufficiently proven, but it requires that he shall state in a plain and correct manner the evidence given in the case and declare and explain the law arising thereon.

6. *Evidence.* Seventy-six cases were reversed because improper evidence was admitted or because proper evidence was excluded, and thirty cases were reversed because the defendant was convicted on insufficient evidence. Most of the reversals grew out of the rules with regard to evidence against self, admission or exclusion of confessions, testimony of codefendants, proof of collateral offenses, character, testimony of husband or wife, newly discovered testimony and insufficient evidence.

7. *Verdicts.* There were nineteen reversals on account of an error in the form of the verdict, and forty-seven on account of an improper judgment on a special verdict. The system of special verdicts has been rather widely used in this state and the rules have not always been clear. But recently the Supreme Court has stated the rules, and practice now is very well established.

8. *Unconstitutional Ordinances or Laws and Jurisdiction.* Fourteen cases were reversed because the defendant was convicted of violating some unconstitutional city ordinance or state law. There were ten reversals which resulted from a conviction in a court not having jurisdiction to hear and determine the case. Most of the cases involv-

ing jurisdiction have grown out of statutory provisions which attempted to vest jurisdiction in some particular court or provide an improper punishment for the offense.

9. *Procedural and Other Errors.* There were a number of reversals on account of procedural errors such as an improperly constituted court, irregular procedure, failure to return verdict in open court, misconduct of the jury and the like. Five cases were reversed because of misconduct of the court and eight because of misconduct of counsel in the trial of the case.

From time to time the General Assembly has passed laws changing criminal procedure in the state. The more glaring defects of criminal procedure appeared during the early days; so the legislature attempted to remedy many of them by statute before this study begins (1890). The Supreme Court has often pointed out specific procedural defects, some of which the legislature has tried to remedy. Important laws have been passed governing appeals, indictments, amendment of warrants, challenges to the jury, statutes of limitations, exclusion of witness by interest or crime, new trial and demurrer to evidence, court stenographers, and addresses of attorneys to the jury. In general it can be said that these laws have tended to simplify procedure and to facilitate the enforcement of criminal law.

The judicial system of North Carolina is not perfect, and it is probably not entirely satisfactory to anybody. From time to time various changes have been suggested, but so far there have been no very sudden or sweeping changes in the judicial process, and it is not likely that there will be in the future. Members of the Bar Association frequently deliver addresses advocating certain changes and reforms in the organization and procedure of the courts, but very few of these are ever enacted into law. Two attempts at reform deserve special consideration: the Commission on Law Reform and Procedure, and the Judicial Conference.

THE COMMISSION ON LAW REFORM AND PROCEDURE

By Legislative Resolution Number 43, 1915, the Commission on Law Reform and Procedure was created. The Commission was composed of five members, Chief Justice Walter Clark being Chairman. The Commission, it seems, went rather carefully over legal procedure in the state and suggested a number of changes in a report which it made to the Governor. Since the report was not adopted by the Legislature we shall not attempt to summarize the recommendations, but there were a few features that should be noted with regard to criminal procedure. We give these suggestions because they indicate some of the points wherein the Commission regarded our procedure as unsatisfactory, and because the suggested changes are interesting. We are not informed as to the dominant motive in the mind of the Commission. We do not know whether the report was expressive of such changes as the Commission really desired or whether it was tempered by the hope of making such recommendations as the Legislature would adopt. The following recommendations were made, with a number of others not given:

1. That expert witnesses shall be selected by the judge and not by the parties, and shall be restricted in number.

2. That in capital cases the State and the prisoner shall each have six peremptory challenges and in all other criminal cases the State and the defendant shall each have two peremptory challenges.

3. The adoption of U. S. Revised Statute, 1024, by which several charges against any person for two or more

acts connected together, or belonging to the same class of crimes, may be joined in one indictment.

4. That the judge shall be reinvested, as before the "Spears Act," with discretion as to the length and number of speeches by counsel, except that in capital cases the number of speeches allowable shall not be less than two on each side, and that each side shall be allowed three hours for argument.

5. The repeal of the provision forbidding any inference in criminal cases to be drawn by the jury from the refusal of the defendant to testify in his own behalf.

Changes in laws governing procedure in the courts come very slowly. In the decade that has elapsed since the report of the Commission not a single recommendation has been adopted *in toto,* but there has been an important change or two in some of the laws. While the Legislature did not adopt the Federal Revised Statute, 1024 as suggested, it did adopt one very similar, immediately following the report, 1917. We give the statute in full:

When there are several charges against any person for the same act or transaction or for two or more acts or transactions connected together, or for two or more transactions of the same class of crimes or offenses, which may be properly joined, instead of several indictments, the whole may be joined in one indictment in separate counts; and if two or more indictments are found in such cases, the court will order them to be consolidated, Provided, this section shall not be construed to reduce the punishment or penalty for such offense or offenses.[2]

The evident purpose of this statute is to simplify indictments and to avoid duplication.

[2] 1917, c. 168; *Consolidated Statutes,* 4622.

THE JUDICIAL CONFERENCE

In 1925 the General Assembly passed an act to create a Judicial Conference for the purpose, as expressed in the statute, of the "continuous study of the organization, rules, and methods of practice and procedure of the judicial system of the state and the practical working and results produced by the system."[3] The Conference is composed of the entire judiciary of the state. This body is composed of the Supreme Court justices, the Superior Court judges, the Attorney General, and one practising attorney from each district, to be appointed by the Governor for a term of two years.[4] Under the original statute there were to be two meetings a year, but upon the recommendation of the Conference itself the Legislature of 1927 amended the act so as to provide for annual meetings only.

At the first meeting of the Conference the work was assigned to six committees as follows:

1. Committee on the Judicial System
2. Committee on Process and Pleadings
3. Committee on Juries
4. Committee on Trials
5. Committee on Appeals
6. Committee on Rules of Practice in the Superior and Supreme Courts

The chairmen of the six committees with the President of the conference, who is the Chief Justice, as chairman ex-officio, constitute the permanent executive committee, thus providing a continuous administrative authority.

At the second meeting of the Conference in Decem-

[3] *Public Laws of North Carolina*, 1925, c. 244 sec. 1.
[4] *Ibid.*, sec. 2.

ber, the various committees filed reports, but of course these reports were merely suggestive and advisory.

Following are some of the suggestions which bear directly upon criminal procedure:

1. The struck jury: This provides that eighteen jurors be drawn and tendered to all parties to the action. When there are more than two antagonistic parties, the number of jurors thus drawn and tendered shall be increased by three jurors for each additional antagonistic party, to be drawn as herein indicated. Each party shall alternately strike three jurors and the remaining twelve jurors shall be empaneled to try the case. If one of the parties fails to strike his three jurors or any of them, the Clerk shall, beginning at the bottom of the list and proceeding toward the first name, in regular order strike enough names to reduce the number of jurors to twelve.

Under the above plans, striking names from the list would of course take the place of peremptory challenges. So the Conference recommended that no peremptory challenges be permitted except in the trial of capital cases.

2. Instead of removing a trial from one county to another as is now done when it appears that the defendant cannot be given a fair trial on account of local prejudices, etc., the Conference recommended that the judge be given authority to summon a jury from another county to try the case.

3. With regard to trials, the committee favored the continuation of the present method of having the judge recapitulate the evidence in charging the jury, and it disapproved the creation of a commission of three physicians who would be subject to call in criminal cases where insanity is pleaded as a defense.

4. In the matter of appeals it was suggested that all statements of cases on appeal be submitted to the trial court and that original exhibits be certified to the Supreme Court without its being necessary to incur the expense of printing exhibits in the brief. It was also suggested that the right of appeal be further limited in certain cases.

5. Another recommendation which appeared to have great promise reads as follows: "That in order to simplify the practice and procedure in the courts of the state and to facilitate the trials of actions, the Supreme Court of North Carolina shall have the power to prescribe by general rules for the Superior Courts and inferior courts of the state, the forms of process, writs, pleadings and motions, and the practice and procedure in all actions."

Certain members of the Conference devoted a great deal of time and energy to the preparation of their report. All the recommendations embodied in the report were placed in the form of a bill for legislative action. But the Legislature rejected the bill in its entirety, except one provision with regard to limiting the time of attorneys for addressing the jury, which was considered in Chapter XI. Perhaps the explanation of the failure of the bill is to be found in the composition of the Legislature itself. In the House of Representatives (1927), of the 120 members, forty-seven were lawyers and three others had studied law. In the Senate out of fifty members thirty-six were lawyers. The committees on the Courts and Judicial Districts and on the Judiciary Numbers 1 and 2 to which the bill was referred were composed largely of practising attorneys. Without prejudice to the bar, it is sufficient to say that as a general rule practising attorneys do not welcome changes in procedure. Whether this attitude is the result of legal study, or whether it is due to the overcrowding of the profession and to direct personal interests is beside the question. The point is that so long as the Legislature is predominated by lawyers we need not expect sweeping and important changes in the direction of simplified procedure.

No attempt will be made to discuss the merits or demerits of any of the proposals submitted by the Conference. It does seem, however, that some of the suggestions are worthy of serious consideration. It is to be hoped that the Judicial Conference is the beginning of better things and that it will be instrumental in bringing about many needed reforms.

TABLE OF CASES

THE UNIVERSITY OF NORTH CAROLINA
SOCIAL STUDY SERIES

UNDER THE GENERAL EDITORSHIP OF HOWARD W. ODUM. BOOKS MARKED WITH * PUBLISHED IN COÖPERATION WITH THE INSTITUTE FOR RESEARCH IN SOCIAL SCIENCE

The University of North Carolina Press, Chapel Hill, N. C.; The Baker and Taylor Co., New York; Oxford University Press, London; The Maruzen Company, Tokyo; Edward Evans & Sons, Ltd., Shanghai.

NCr